Do-It-Yourself
Publicity

DO-IT-YOURSELF
PUBLICITY

DAVID F. RAMACITTI

amacom

American Management Association

This book is available at a special discount when ordered in bulk quantities. For information, contact Special Sales Department, AMACOM, a division of American Management Association, 135 West 50th Street, New York, NY 10020.

This publication is designed to provide accurate and authoritative information in regard to the subject matter covered. It is sold with the understanding that the publisher is not engaged in rendering legal, accounting, or other professional service. If legal advice or other expert assistance is required, the services of a competent professional person should be sought.

Library of Congress Cataloging-in-Publication Data

Ramacitti, David F.
    Do-it-yourself publicity / David F. Ramacitti.
        p.   cm.
    Includes bibliographical references.
    ISBN 0-8144-5982-X
    ISBN 0-8144-7773-9 (pbk.)
    1 Public relations.   2. Publicity.   I. Title.
    HD59.R18   1990   89-81026
    659—dc20   CIP

First AMACOM paperback edition 1991.

Printing number

10   9   8   7   6   5   4   3   2   1

This book is dedicated to two people:

To Patsy, who is many things to me,
but most important of all,
my wife and friend;

And, to Dr. Reef Waldrop, my former journalism professor at Western Illinois University, who taught me that
writing is a most extraordinary adventure.

Contents

Do-It-Yourself
Publicity

Introduction

O nce upon a time, editors, like characters out of a Jimmy Stewart movie, could spend lots of time with their feet up on the desk, puffing their pipes and chatting with friends and neighbors about the goings-on around town. No event was so small that it did not deserve some space in the news columns.

But those days are long gone! A visit to a modern newspaper or television news operation would be more like a trip into To-morrowland. Instead of listening to the clatter of typewriters, you'd hear the whir of computer discs receiving a nonstop flow of national and international news via satellite. Instead of seeing an irascible, Lou Grant type shouting at harried reporters, you'd be more likely to find editors and news directors sorting through computer-generated menus of the thousands of news stories and features available to them each day, wondering how they will find the news columns or airtime to run even a tenth of the material.

Competition for the attention of the public is intense and is growing more so by the day. Advertising is on billboards, radio, television, videocassettes, and in movies, newspapers, magazines, shoppers, posters; it even arrives in the mail. All these claim that their products are vitally important, indispensable, newer, better, faster, sexier. . . . Various authorities estimate that the average consumer is bombarded by several hundred to a thousand advertising messages per day! And this doesn't even include the editorial portions of the newspapers and magazines or the news broadcasts and documentaries on television and radio that we *choose* to pay attention to.

So how can your small business, professional or service office, human service or charitable agency, or volunteer club hope to compete in this media melee for its fair share of the public's attention? You can compete by learning to use the fundamental techniques of generating publicity in the media and adapting them to the special needs of your organization.

This book will:

- Familiarize you with the basic techniques and tools of publicity.
- Teach you to adapt these basic tools and techniques to your specific situation.
- Stimulate ideas for news releases and other publicity projects that do not require large amounts of out-of-pocket cash.
- Familiarize you with the strengths and weaknesses of the various media, so that you can use them effectively to achieve your publicity goals.
- Get you started on developing a complete media list for your community and/or industry.
- Help you to write a basic do-it-yourself publicity plan for your organization, even if the plan is little more than some notes on the back of an envelope.

THE VIEWPOINT

Every book has a viewpoint. Authors make assumptions about who their readers are and what they need and want to know. About this book's readers, I assume that:

- You are a small or growing business: a retail shop, a machine shop, an appliance repair shop, a bed and breakfast operation, a delivery service, a franchise fast food outlet, a woodworking shop, a hobby shop, an independent auto repair shop. . . .
- Or you are part of the explosion of small professional service firms: dentists, attorneys, architects, optometrists, chiropractors, computer software consultants (or, for that matter, consultants in any field you can think of, from waste management to music therapy), temporary services agencies, housecleaning or landscaping services, executive placement firms, insurance offices, real estate brokers, financial services counselors. . . .

• Or you are part of the vast array of nonprofit human service agencies and groups: the United Way or a United Way member agency, the Salvation Army, Goodwill, or an agency dealing with adoptions, family or marriage counseling, drug abuse, youth services, teen pregnancy, outreach, neighborhood advocacy, displaced worker support,. . . .

• Or you are part of the extensive network of small, local health support agencies whose activities range from fund-raising to the delivery of client services and family support: Easter Seals, the Association for Retarded Citizens, Muscular Dystrophy, the March of Dimes, the Red Cross. . . .

• Or you are a member of one of the millions of volunteer clubs and organizations spread across the country: from service clubs to garden clubs, from bridge clubs to bicycle clubs, from bowling leagues to Little Leagues, from chambers of commerce to chamber music lovers, from wilderness backpackers to urban architecture buffs. . . .

And that all of you need, want, and deserve more positive media exposure for your business, agency, or group than you are now receiving.

About your needs, I assume:

- You do not have the funds to hire a public relations agency, nor do you have a professional public relations person on your staff.
- All of your publicity activities will be arranged on a do-it-yourself basis by someone in your business or organization.
- That person does not have a background in journalism or communications.
- Most of the time you will be dealing with *local media* or your own trade publications and will have only limited contact, if any, with the national networks or big-time newspapers or magazines.

Certainly the practice of public relations, especially at the national or international level, has become very sophisticated and complex. In this book, I've chosen to oversimplify and to stress the fundamentals. The approach is very how-to-oriented. I've tried to give a good many practical, action-oriented suggestions: specific things you can do tomorrow morning when you get to your office, shop, or plant. I've provided lots of basic rules and checklists that are designed to get you started as quickly as possible generating positive public exposure for your group, agency, or business.

Some of the topics covered are:

- What a news release is and how to write one that will get the attention of the media—and no, you don't have to be able to write like Ernest Hemingway to produce a news release.
- How to put together a successful news conference—and no, you don't need the President of the United States or even Robert Redford as the star attraction to get the media to come.
- Enough ideas for generating news releases so that even the smallest business could send one out on a weekly basis if it really wanted to.
- Why the local newspaper's centuries-old roots in the printing and news business definitely work *for* you in your quest for more media exposure and, conversely, why the electronic media's roots in the entertainment industry tend to work against you.
- Why you will be making a serious mistake if you focus all your media planning on the traditional major media in your community (the daily newspaper, TV and radio stations) and ignore the "little" media: the neighborhood "throwaways," the retiree newsletters, the community weekly, the high school or college papers, the specialized radio stations and cable channels, the public broadcasting channel. . . .
- How to survive—and perhaps even turn the tables in your favor—when some sort of controversy does erupt and the media are after your hide.
- Why you should appear as a guest on every local talk show that'll book you, as often as they'll book you, and what to do to be at your most articulate and relaxed best when they do.
- Why a comprehensive media file can be worth its weight in gold and how to get one started.
- How to write and implement a publicity or media plan for your business, agency, or group, even if it's little more than three goals jotted down on the back of an envelope.

PUBLIC RELATIONS VS. PUBLICITY VS. PAID ADS

It's also important for you to understand that this book focuses almost entirely on one specific aspect of public relations, that is, on generating free publicity for your small business or group in the various kinds of media that are available to you. This is as opposed to paid advertising, which is probably what comes to mind first when the topic of promoting your business or group comes up.

Certainly paid advertising plays an important role in the promotional plans of many kinds of businesses, especially retail businesses, where the competition is intense. Yet one of the recurring themes of this book is that most businesses and groups are hardly scratching the surface when it comes to exploiting the opportunities for, and the benefits of, a positive publicity program on behalf of their organization.

Don't confuse public relations with publicity. You will often hear these terms used as if they were synonymous. They're not.

Publicity is news coverage by the media of the products, services, activities, events, positions, people, contributions, history, or goals and dreams of your business, agency, or group. This can include traditional news stories in the newspapers or on radio or television as well as articles in magazines and other publications and appearances on talk and public service shows.

Public relations is an umbrella term that includes not only the programs designed to generate free publicity but also many different projects and activities that have little or nothing to do with the media—like developing brochures and fliers, publishing a customer newsletter, hosting seminars and workshops, sponsoring an open house or annual meeting, developing exhibitions and shows and staging all sorts of special events, such as golf tournaments or parades and, yes, even those lavish cocktail parties or sit-down dinners for VIPs!

YOUR LOVE/HATE RELATIONSHIP WITH THE MEDIA

Finally, there is a strange, almost paradoxical, love/hate relationship between the media and public relations practitioners for which you should have some appreciation.

On the one hand, journalists in all fields place a great deal of value on maintaining their objectivity and independence. So, to keep from compromising that independence, they work hard at keeping an arm's-length relationship with those who seek coverage in their respective media. This applies especially to those who are trying to obtain this coverage as paid professionals, for instance, public relations firms or the PR staff members of a business or government agency.

On the other hand, as every working editor and news director knows, there is never a sufficiently large staff to cover every news event, to dig out and write every feature story, to provide the necessary background on every issue or topic of importance, let alone stay on top of the myriad of activities that occur daily in every community, big or small. The fact is, today's daily or weekly newspaper, today's evening TV newscast, today's hourly radio news roundup would not, indeed could not, exist as we know them without a regular and significant influx of information from non-staff sources!

The irony of it is that they—the media—need you—the seeker of publicity—as much as you need them! Of course they are the gatekeepers of your access to the audiences they provide. At the same time, you are a major source of the information they must provide to keep that audience's attention.

In other words, in your relationships with media people you should never allow yourself to be cast in the role of the beggar who seeks some sort of special dispensation for your business, agency, or group. As I will point out particularly in the following chapter and will stress again and again throughout this book, you have a perfectly legitimate right to far more coverage than you've probably ever gotten or, for that matter, ever imagined you could get. If there is a single driving theme of this book, it is "Go for it!"

1

Twelve Good Reasons Why You Should Think About Publicity

It's unfortunate but true that many small businesses still have the attitude "Just leave me alone and let me do my thing." They do not seek or welcome attention from any outsiders, especially if the outsiders are the media, the government, or some kind of consumer or advocacy group. It's the classic head-in-the-sand approach: "Maybe if I ignore them, they'll go away." Perhaps there was a time when the marketplace tolerated this kind of fiercely independent attitude. But that time is past.

Today's marketplace is no longer merely competitive; it is hypercompetitive! The shelves and racks of our stores and malls are loaded with dozens of "me too" products. Bankers now sell insurance and insurance salespeople now offer CDs. Did you ever expect to see the day when hospitals would advertise on billboards and television, like Coca-Cola or McDonald's?

Why should your small business, agency, or group worry about getting good publicity? Is it really worth all the time and hassle? There are at least a dozen very good reasons why you should generate as much favorable publicity for your business, agency, or group as you possibly can:

1. *It is simply a smart dollars and cents investment in promoting your organization.* Whether you measure your "profit" in terms of dollars left over after expenses are paid or in terms of more contributions, more members, or more clients served, promoting your organization's name and activities is no longer an optional "it would be nice if" task; it's critical to your survival!

7

Every positive article or photo published in the daily newspaper, every favorable one-minute clip on the early evening news, every complimentary mention in some specialty newsletter or magazine is FREE! Sure, it may cost a little bit of staff time, some duplicating and postage expense. But it did not cost you anywhere near the big bucks that the same number of column inches in the newspaper or the same amount of airtime on the TV news would have cost if you'd paid for it as advertising!

For example, a half-page ad—which is about what a good-sized feature story will run in a local daily newspaper—will cost at least $500 to $600 in a small-town daily, perhaps $1,500 in a newspaper in a medium-size market, and as much as $3,000 or $5,000 in a large metropolitan newspaper. A one-minute story on the TV late evening news will run you $200 to $250 in a small market, $500 to $1,000 or more in a medium market, and $2,500 to $4,000 in a large urban market.

There is a major state tourism promotion bureau that spends most of its budget on writing and sending out its own news releases and on bringing in travel writers and editors for "familiarization" tours to generate articles and feature stories about the state's attractions. Over the years, this bureau has kept records of the articles and TV features that have appeared and it estimates that there has been about a 4 to 1 benefit to cost ratio. In other words, if the tourism bureau had paid for the editorial space and airtime it has received, like advertising, it would have cost four times as much as it has spent on the news releases, media kits, and "fam" tours. That's not a bad return on investment.

2. *You get more "bang for the buck" in terms of audience attention with editorial coverage.* This is a kind of corollary to number 1, the opposite side of the same coin; only here the focus is on audience attention rather than on dollars spent. What I'm suggesting is that on an inch-for-inch basis (using print media) or a minute-for-minute basis (using electronic media), you'll get far more reader or viewer attention from free editorial space or time than you will from an equal amount of paid ad space or time.

Just think for a moment about how you read newspapers and magazines or watch television or listen to the radio. If you're like most people, you read most of the articles (or at least the headlines) in the newspaper but at the same time, skip over the ads.

That is, unless you're specifically looking for something: You need tires and someone is having a tire sale; you've been thinking you need a new sportcoat and your favorite shop has announced its new spring arrivals; only then do you notice the ads. Or you watch the TV news stories with interest but pick up the paper and read a few paragraphs or carry on a conversation with your spouse or go to the kitchen (or bathroom) during the commercials! Sound familiar?

I know of a small manufacturer of a specialty garden tool who has tried display ads in various gardening magazines, but finds he gets two, three or more times the results—in terms of inquiries or actual orders—from just one mention in one of those same magazines' new products columns!

3. *It's just good sense to build your "bank account of goodwill" with the media and the community.* If it's true we've moved into a new era of competitiveness in the marketplace, perhaps it's only slightly less true to say that we're also entering a new era of contentiousness in our organizational and personal relationships. Individuals and organizations seem willing to sue one another at the drop of a hat. Advocacy and special interest groups, with their confrontational approach to everything, sprout with the ease of dandelions. Legislators promulgate laws that run to 1,000 and more pages. And regulatory agencies issue voluminous and highly technical manuals of rules and regulations on practically a daily basis.

What seems to be emerging is a new expectation of corporate and institutional accountability on the part of the public. Perhaps it's the long-term fallout from Watergate, Bhopal, Three Mile Island, and other disasters in which there was a perception that the politicians or corporations involved were less than open and honest in their dealings with the public and the media. This perception contrasts especially with the public's highly favorable attitude toward Johnson & Johnson after that company's enlightened handling of the Tylenol tampering case in 1982.

It seems clear that if it hasn't happened already, we are certainly nearing the end of the time when even small local businesses or organizations can get away with the attitude "Just leave me alone to do my thing." Sooner or later, every business or organization is going to need something from the community: a zoning change to put up a new building, a variance on a sign ordinance, a city (or county or state) economic development grant (or loan guarantee) to create more jobs, a long-term lease to use city property for storage purposes, permission for a new curb cut, or an extension to a street or alley to improve access to its property.

All these "needs" involve an approval process that almost invariably includes a public hearing, with the opportunity for interested or affected parties to have their say. Very often that "say" takes the form of virulent and totally unexpected opposition. I'm not suggesting that a regular publicity program for your business or agency or group will guarantee that you'll never be faced with neighborhood opposition to your request to rezone a piece of property so that you can build an addition to your building or that some local advocacy group will never issue a critical statement to the media finding fault with one of your policies or procedures.

What I do suggest very strongly is that a diligently conducted publicity program that regularly generates favorable coverage in the media is like building a bank account of goodwill. Even if it can't altogether head off any given controversy—and, anyway, how would you ever know if it did?—it may well mean that you'll at least get less hostile, and perhaps even favorable, treatment in the media, which in turn means less harsh treatment in the court of public opinion.

4. *You simply have a right to more media coverage.* As a legitimate organization that involves people and interacts with the community, you simply have a right to more space or airtime than you are probably now receiving. It's part of the fundamental openness of the democratic process. The fact is, most businesses or organizations do not get their fair share of media exposure; usually because they haven't bothered to tell the media about the interesting things they're doing.

When I was a newspaper reporter, I always looked forward to doing feature articles on local businesses for the traditional year-end special section—we called ours the "progress edition." I was constantly amazed at the many fascinating and previously untold story ideas I discovered in virtually every business or organization I visited. When I would tell the folks at the business, "This is a

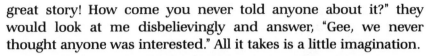
great story! How come you never told anyone about it?" they would look at me disbelievingly and answer, "Gee, we never thought anyone was interested." All it takes is a little imagination.

5. *It's free!* For some organizations the free publicity that is available through the media may be the only way they can afford to reach the public. This is especially true for the many nonprofit agencies and/or volunteer groups that don't have large budgets and for some small start-up businesses.

Charles A. Hillestad, who, with his wife, is the owner of the Queen Anne Inn, says he used "audacious" public relations to help launch their ten-room bed and breakfast operation near downtown Denver, Colorado, according to an article in *Marketing News.**

Hillestad was able to generate mentions of his inn in such prestigious publications as the *New York Times,* as well as in *Inc., Elle,* and *Bridal Guide* magazines. Among the various "tricks" he used to generate free publicity was sending articles about the inn to travel magazines. But he went beyond just the travel publications by customizing articles to the specific editorial approach of each magazine, for instance, by focusing on the inn's antiques for an antiques magazine.

6. *It's more believable.* Even if your organization can afford to and does use paid advertising as a promotional tool, you should still make the maximum possible use of publicity. Why? People simply have more faith in what they read in the editorial columns of a newspaper or magazine and in what they hear from TV or radio commentators than they have in paid advertising. News is more believable than ads.

7. *You can sell products through publicity.* Sales pitches are by no means limited to paid advertising. Just look at how effectively the travel and hospitality industry has used publicity as a sales tool. Make no mistake about it, all those "rah rah" feature articles about fun places to go and all those favorable restaurant reviews in the newspapers and magazines are most certainly "selling" you on those spots as somewhere you should visit.

What's more sales-oriented than a direct-mail catalog? It's

* Vol. 22, No. 14 (July 4, 1988), p. 1.

nothing but page after page of ads for some company's products, right? Yet look at the Patagonia catalog for the highly successful outdoor clothing and equipment mail-order house. You'll find page after page of "articles" written by staff members and customers about how and where they used the equipment rather than the more conventional photos or drawings accompanied by a description of the product and the price. Patagonia catalogs are avidly read and jealously guarded, more like a treasured magazine than just another mail-order catalog.

8. *Publicity can even generate revenue, make money for you.* More than one organization has successfully converted its free-distribution newsletter, originally published as a public relations tool, into paid subscriptions. This has been a particularly successful approach in the health and fitness industry.

In addition, there is always the possibility of putting together a collection of articles you've generated into a pamphlet or booklet and marketing it. For example, this might work well for a how-to business, such as a hardware store or home center. Finally, sometimes you can even get paid for writing an article for a magazine or journal, especially if you have some unique expertise to offer.

9. *Regular exposure in the media legitimizes your business, group, or agency in the eyes of the community.* There is a subtle but nonetheless very real perception people have that if something's in the paper or on TV it must be important. The media themselves foster and promote this attitude because it makes their role seem more important, more indispensable.

If your name shows up regularly in a positive way in the media, it helps pave the way for when your business goes to see the bank for an expansion loan or when your agency launches an endowment fund drive or when your club is looking for sponsors for a youth fitness festival you're planning. Regular mentions in the media say to the community, "We're here to stay. We're not some fly-by-night outfit that's here today and gone tomorrow. We're neighbors, part of the community."

10. *It can help you recruit good employees.* You might think this item ought to be included under the last one, but actually it deserves stand-alone status because it's going to become increasingly important in the years ahead. Changing demographics and

life-styles suggest that in the 1990s and beyond there will be increasing shortages of skilled and experienced workers in many fields.

So, when you run your ads in the classified section for the people you need to hire in order to expand and grow, what's their reaction going to be? Are they going to recall reading and hearing positive things about your firm and think, "Yeah, that'd be a good place to work. You can get ahead there; they always seem to be promoting people. They seem to be interested in their employees. Wasn't there something in the paper about a new training program?" Or is their reaction going to be something like "Why would I want to work there? I've never heard of them."

11. *You can do it yourself.* If you don't have a background in marketing and promotional work, successfully generating favorable exposure through news releases is easier to accomplish on a do-it-yourself basis than through paid advertising. A paid ad campaign, especially if it involves a highly competitive marketplace and extensive use of mass media, requires a good deal of sophistication to be effective.

12. *You can become a media "source."* Finally, it's simply a good idea to develop relationships with the media in the same way that it's a good idea to develop other kinds of friendships in the community. Today's buzzword for this is "networking."

The fact is, writers and reporters are always on the lookout for "sources," especially at the local level. Certainly "sources" can tip a reporter off to some major scandal, which is the way we've been conditioned to think of "sources" by the national media. However, for most reporters, nine out of ten of their "sources" are people in various specialized fields whom they have come to know and trust and whom they call on for background information to help them understand a complex issue they're reporting on. In many cases, the "source" may not even be quoted directly in the story.

Just think of the important influence you could have, even if it's indirect, on how the media reports information vital to your field if you've been able to develop a trusted relationship with a reporter, if you've become an "expert" upon whom he or she relies.

Getting Started Tomorrow Morning

Go back over the twelve reasons given for why you should be thinking about generating more publicity for your business, agency, or group. On a legal pad, do some brainstorming as to how each of those twelve reasons might be relevant to the specific needs of your business or organization. Don't worry about form at this point; just write down as many thoughts and ideas as you can.

Here are some questions to stimulate your thinking:

- When's the last time the name of your business, agency, or group was mentioned in a positive way in any medium?
- Do you know anyone in the media? Which media? What does that person do?
- How much do you spend on paid media advertising to promote your business or group? What if you could double the effectiveness of those dollars?
- Think of at least three positive things that you accomplished or that happened to your business or agency or group within the past year. How much publicity did you get on each?
- Now think about any negative things that happened. How much publicity did they get?
- Now think about any *potentially* positive things you could do and how much publicity they could generate.
- Conversely, think about any *potentially* negative things that could happen to your business, agency, or group and what kind of publicity they could generate.

Set aside your notes for the time being. But save them because you'll want to use them again later.

2

Fifty Excuses for
Sending Out a News Release

There are far fewer news releases sent out by small businesses, small agencies, and volunteer clubs and organizations than there should be! Remember the old TV series "The Naked City"? It was a show about New York cops, and it always ended with one of the cops saying, "There are eight million stories in the naked city. This has been one of them."

Your business, agency, or organization is like that. There are lots and lots of interesting things happening all around you every day that really deserve a news release. You probably take them for granted—"Oh, they wouldn't be interested in that!"—simply because you're so familiar with them.

In fact, it's my opinion that virtually any small business, agency, or club could legitimately send out a *minimum* of six news releases per year, and that many could easily double that number. Of course, not all these ideas will get you a banner headline on page one or the lead story on the late news. Some will only get a two- or three-line brief on the business page.

The point is that in today's increasingly competitive marketplace you should be taking advantage of every opportunity available to you to receive positive public exposure. Especially if it doesn't cost you anything.

Here's a checklist of fifty reasons for sending out a news release. Certainly not all apply to every business, agency, or group. But the list will provide some guideposts for you when you generate ideas applicable to your specific organization. Send out a news release when:

1. You start up a new business or establish a new agency or group. The more unique or unusual it is, the better.
2. The anniversary (fifth, tenth, twentieth) of your business, agency, or group rolls around. It's something to celebrate.
3. Your CEO has served fifteen, twenty, or more years.
4. You want to release a summary of your annual report to stockholders, customers, clients, contributors, or members. You should issue some form of annual report even if your business is a sole proprietorship.
5. You elect new board members and/or officers of the board.
6. You issue a position statement regarding some community, national, legislative, or industry issue, as when you oppose a proposed new tax because it's unfair to small business or when you support a local school bond issue.
7. A major milestone for your business, agency, or group is reached, such as the 100,000th customer or the attainment of a major fund-raising goal.
8. You meet some unusual challenge or rise above adversity, especially if the challenge is posed by external forces, such as your customers or the government. These are the "They said it couldn't be done, but we did it!" stories. "Our customers demanded 99.9 percent reliability, far beyond the industry standard, and we delivered." "A major warehouse fire at one of our largest customer's plants destroyed their entire stock. By working around the clock, we were able to resupply them in seven days."
9. There is any personnel change, such as a promotion, retirement, or new hire, at a supervisory or management level. Be sure to include a good head-and-shoulders photo.
10. An employee or volunteer has retired after a long career, say, after fifteen or more years of service.
11. The ownership status of your business has changed, whether this means merging with another business, purchasing or being purchased by another concern, or taking on a partner or major new investor(s). Of course, this applies to mergers or reorganizations of agencies and volunteer groups as well.

12. A new generation steps into the family business, by inheritance or purchase of the ownership or simply by entering the business on a lower level. The continuity of the generations is the story.
13. A new executive director or CEO is hired.
14. Your business lands a major new customer, such as a large government contract.
15. New jobs are created, especially when there are a lot of them.
16. New supervisory or executive positions are created.
17. Your present physical facilities are expanded, for instance, by way of a new building, increased office space, a larger showroom, an enlarged warehouse, modernized shipping/receiving docks, or additional manufacturing space.
18. Your business installs some type of pollution control equipment or revises old practices or procedures so as to eliminate an adverse environmental impact, especially when this is done on a voluntary basis. A small Midwest foundry got national press attention when, instead of shipping its spent foundry sand to a landfill, it worked out a deal with a local cement quarry whereby the waste materials would be used in making new concrete.
19. You have undertaken a major renovation or redecoration of your present buildings or grounds, especially if you've restored a dilapidated or rundown historic building for use as a bed and breakfast facility or as law offices or as a unique retail shop.
20. You have purchased major new equipment or machinery, especially if it's high tech, such as new diagnostic equipment at a health clinic or a high-precision laser metal cutter for your manufacturing plant.
21. You have been certified by a major buyer; for instance, as the owner of a local machine shop, you have been certified as a preferred supplier to John Deere or Boeing.
22. You have taken your business, agency, or group in a new direction or "repositioned" it, as when Rotary International began to admit women.
23. You have opened a second store locally or established a warehouse or manufacturing facility in another area.

24. Your business, group, or agency has introduced a product line or service. For instance, your clothing store has added a new brand of women's wear to its merchandise, or your retiree's club is now going to schedule two or three bus trips a year for its members.

25. There is a major change in customer policies or procedures. A small, local department store got considerable local publicity, and even some national media attention, a few years ago when it dropped all interest charges on house charge accounts.

26. You have set up advisory groups, user groups, or some other customer/client/member-involvement mechanism, such as installing an 800 customer service hotline.

27. You have undertaken a major improvement or enhancement of your products or services, as when a manufacturer switches to a new high-tech material that doubles his product's life expectancy, or when a law firm hires paralegals to expedite its caseload.

28. You have developed and/or adopted a new manufacturing or design innovation that results in higher productivity or reduced cost or a better product, such as introducing computer-driven quality-control devices.

29. Outsiders visit your plant to learn about and inspect the innovation you've introduced, as when a delegation from overseas visits to see a new robotic device you've developed.

30. You want to announce the results of product research you have conducted.

31. One of your products or services has its twenty-fifth, thirtieth, or fiftieth anniversary. Just think of the strong positive images you can create with this theme: Here's a tried and true, thoroughly market-proven product or service, the industry standard! Your competitors will be green with envy.

32. You have acquired an exclusive franchise to a product, brand, or service in your area. For instance, you have been named the only Acura auto dealer in town, or you have been selected by a government agency to develop a pilot

program for helping minorities to start their own businesses.

33. Your business, agency, or group has received an award, recognition, commendation, or accreditation from a professional or trade organization, the government, or even the community. For instance, your local chamber of commerce may be among the minority of local chambers to have been accredited by the U.S. Chamber of Commerce.

34. An individual in your group, agency, or business has received an award, recognition, commendation, or accreditation from a trade or professional association, the government, or the community. This might include an insurance person who is named a Charter Life Underwriter, a physician who is admitted to one of the "colleges" for a specialty, a realtor who has made the Million Dollar Roundtable, or a social worker who becomes an Accredited Clinical Social Worker. Virtually every occupation or profession has some form of recognition of achievement.

35. Your business, agency, or group presents an award or other recognition to an employee, member, or client—the employee of the month, the rehabilitant of the year, the top salesperson.

36. You are visited by a VIP, whether that VIP is a public figure or someone from within your industry. A small, local bicycle shop generated a lengthy newspaper feature story and coverage on two out of three local evening newscasts when the president of a major Japanese bicycle manufacturing company visited his store as part of a U.S. tour. And remember, a VIP does not always have to be human to become news! A local Midwest garden club garnered lots of media attention when it "borrowed" a popular baby elephant from the local zoo as its "star attraction" at a lawn and garden show.

37. Your group, business, or agency—or any individual in it— is asked to make a presentation, deliver testimony, or participate in a symposium by a professional or government organization. The more national in scope the subject is, the better.

38. An individual in your business, group, or agency is named to serve in a leadership position in a major community or charitable group. For instance, your CEO is asked to serve as the United Way campaign chairman or to be a member of the mayor's special task force on updating the city's zoning ordinances.

39. An individual in your business, group, or agency is named to serve in a leadership position in a local, state, or national professional group or association, as when one of your firm's partners is elected president of the state CPA organization.

40. Your retail business is staging a major sale, especially when that sale will be accompanied by some unique event or promotion, such as staying open all night for the first time.

41. Your business sponsors a significant community festival or event open to the general public, as when your stamp and coin shop is the major sponsor of a philatelic show and charity auction at the community center.

42. You are sponsoring a workshop, seminar, symposium, or product demonstration, as when you have several manufacturers' representatives come to your retail store on a specific Saturday to demonstrate new products and answer customer questions.

43. You want to publish the results of surveys or questionnaires you have conducted of the community or industry. Every January a local temporary employment agency conducts a survey of area businesses about their plans for adding jobs in the coming year. The results of the survey often get page one coverage.

44. You have made projections about future business trends, as when a local utility issues data on future energy needs.

45. You have made projections about future community needs. For example, a local bicycle club might survey the community's interest in health and fitness and discover the need for a fitness program geared to seniors.

46. You can show how your business premises, products, or customers have changed over the years, especially when you have old-time photos or documents to help illustrate

the story. Newspapers and local magazines really go for nostalgia features.

47. There have been changes in your agency's services and/or clients over the years. Again, it helps to have nostalgic photos or artifacts—for example, of the 1920s settlement house that's become a modern family counseling agency, or of the Civil War era orphanage that's become a residential center for emotionally disturbed youth.

48. There have been changes in your group's activities and/or membership over the years—for instance, the hunting club that's turned into an influential conservation group, the ladies' garden society that's grown into a major botanical center, the small community band that used to play Sunday afternoon concerts in the park that's become a regional symphony orchestra.

49. Employees or members of your business, agency, or group are involved in a charitable or community service activity; for instance, volunteers from your staff pay for and install playground equipment in a nearby park or help a fellow employee rebuild his house after it was severely damaged by fire.

50. Your business, agency, or group is caught up in some out-of-the-ordinary or unique happening involving its employees, customers, clients, or members.

You may have noticed two things about these suggestions, two patterns or themes that are constant.

First, all of them are basically positive and upbeat. One of my assumptions is that you should be generating news releases that present your business, agency, or group in the best possible light to your customers, clients, contributors, or the community at large. That's why throughout most of this book I stress positive publicity opportunities. However, there are times—hopefully rare for most of you—when you will have to deal with controversy and adverse publicity. What you should do in these circumstances is covered in Chapter 10.

Second, most of these suggestions have a strong undercurrent of the unique, the special, the unusual. There is an old saw in journalism: If a dog bites a man, that's not news, since that's what dogs are supposed to do; but if a man bites a dog, that's news! The better you can convey the uniqueness or unusualness of your news item to the media, the more likely you are to get their attention, to generate more coverage.

THE GEE WHIZ FACTOR

No checklist can be all encompassing as to the occasions on which you should or should not prepare a press release. So use what I call the gee whiz factor to test the potential newsworthiness—the likelihood that your release will be used in the newspaper or on the air—of any idea you have for a news release.

Briefly outline your story idea to several friends, preferably people who are not intimately involved with your organization or its industry on a regular basis.

If the reaction of most of them is "Gee whiz, I didn't know that," or words to that effect, then you can assume that an editor or news director will also be likely to find the item of interest to his or her readers or viewers.

On the other hand, if the reaction you get is something like "Yeah, and the sun came up today," then it's a safe bet that your idea is what editors and news directors would call "nonnews" and you should save your time and energy.

The reason you ought to test your ideas on people who have little or no background in your group or business or agency is that you know too much about it! You're not objective. Your day-to-day familiarity with your equipment or operations or what have you means that you start to take them for granted. We all have a tendency to assume that because we know all about something, everybody else does too. But "everybody" doesn't know!

Getting Started Tomorrow Morning

First, for a week or so take the daily newspaper and turn to the city (or local news) page or the business page. See if you can match the articles that appear on these pages with one of the fifty suggestions

I've listed. This is an exercise to help sensitize you to looking for story ideas within your own organization, to help you develop what reporters call a "nose for news."

Second, go back over the list of fifty story ideas and think about each one in the context of your business, agency, or group. On a legal pad, jot down brief notes for specific story ideas about *your* business, agency, or group that one of my suggestions may have inspired. Don't worry about style at this point; just get the idea down as quickly as you can.

How many ideas do you have? It wouldn't surprise me if you came up with at least two dozen or more. If you don't have a minimum of a dozen, try again.

Now test some of these ideas on your friends for the gee whiz factor. My prediction is that you'll be surprised at how many of your ideas do, in fact, produce a positive gee whiz reaction. Save these notes as well. We'll use them again later.

3

News Releases:
The Hammer and
Saw of Publicity

L ike the carpenter's hammer and saw, the news release is the basic tool of any public relations program. Just as a carpenter could build a simple but acceptable shelter with just a hammer and saw, you can put together a basic but functional public relations program just using news releases. The fact is, some public relations programs can be conducted entirely on the basis of news releases. Indeed, no matter what else you do, from direct mailings to mounting a parade down Main Street, you ought to have at least one news release in your campaign.

In this chapter, I'll explore the four basic kinds of news releases and discuss the media kit. In the next chapter, I'll talk about how to write a news release and get into those famous Five W's—the who, what, where, when, and why—of any story.

THE FOUR KINDS OF RELEASES

There are four basic kinds of news releases:

1. *The advance or announcement.* This is by far the most common type of news release; probably six out of every ten news releases are advances or announcements. Its purpose is simply to announce some event or activity. It tends to be topical and time-sensitive. That is, it doesn't make much sense to announce an

event after it's over. A sample advance news release can be seen in Figure 3-1.

The advance is the kind of news release you use to:

- Let people know that your retail store will be hosting an open house next month.
- Announce that your software development firm will soon be issuing a new, advanced update of its popular small business accounting program.
- Inform everyone that your charitable group will be holding a fund-raising costume dance on Halloween.
- Take a position on some issue, for instance, that your business or organization supports a proposed school bond issue.
- Announce that your real estate agency will host a free seminar on property as an investment.
- Let folks know that your dog obedience club is scheduling a dog show.
- Announce that your hospital will be giving free blood pressure checks next week at the senior center.
- Tell everyone that your insurance agency is the local sponsor for a national safety poster contest for school children.

2. *The backgrounder.* This kind of news release generally provides detailed or in-depth background information on an issue, a product, a business, or an organization. It tends to be serious in tone and longer in length and less time-sensitive than an advance. Figure 3-2 is a sample backgrounder news release.

This type of news release is often issued all by itself. For example, when your business is having its twenty-fifth or fiftieth anniversary, you might issue a news release that traces its development and growth over the years.

A backgrounder might present a local angle on some issue that's hot at the national level, for example, if the chemistry department at the local college is doing research on acid rain, or if the director of a local human services agency served in the Peace Corps in an area that's just experienced a major earthquake.

Backgrounders also deal with the changing seasons. Early in the spring, a local garden shop might issue a report about local

Figure 3-1. Sample of an announcement or advance news release.

FROM: Mary Smith, Publicity Chairman
       Southside Airedale Society
       123 5th St.
       Hometown, Minnesota
       Days 555-1234 / Eve. 555-5678

FOR RELEASE AT WILL

RENOWNED OBEDIENCE EXPERT TO SPEAK

Mr. Sidney R. Doe, author of *The 30-Day Dog Training Book*, the world's best-selling dog obedience training book, will speak to the Southside Airedale Society's monthly meeting March 21, at 7:30 P.M. at the Community Center, 222 Main St., Hometown.

The meeting is open to the public. All dog owners, regardless of breed, are invited to attend. There is no charge for admission. However, voluntary contributions will be accepted for refreshments following the talk.

# # #

soil and moisture conditions after the winter and what to do to get ready for spring planting.

Sometimes this type of release is issued in combination with others. For instance, if your manufacturing firm has just landed a NASA contract to build a new telemetry instrument for the space shuttle, you would probably focus on the specific instrument to be built for NASA in one release, but, at the same time, issue a second release that provides background information on how your firm has been building instruments for the aerospace industry since the Korean War.

Or, if you hire a new school superintendent, the initial announcement of the selection would include all the pertinent data about his or her experience and qualifications, but you might also issue a backgrounder that discusses the intensive selection procedure and how various elements of the community were included in the process.

Or, if your bicycle club announced its new policy that riders

Figure 3-2.   Example of a backgrounder news release.

FROM: Greater Suburba Board of Realtors
        Sam Winters, President
        Winters Realty
        543 1st St.
        Suburba, New York
        Off. 555-4321 / Res. 555-9876

FOR IMMEDIATE RELEASE

WHY COMMUNITY SUPPORT FOR SUBURBA'S NEW SCHOOL BOND
ISSUE IS VITAL

The city of Suburba was founded as a village in 1947, just one
of the hundreds and hundreds of new communities that were
springing up on the outskirts of larger, more established cities in
the years immediately following World War II. At the end of 1948,
Suburba's population was estimated at just over 1,100. The decen-
nial U.S. Census figures tell the story of Suburba's phenomenal
growth:

        1950— 5,057
        1960—18,667
        1970—31,988
        1980—44,007
        1985—48,430 (estimate)

The first public building built in Suburba was not a village hall
but an elementary school. It opened its doors to over 300 children
in the fall of 1948. Between 1948 and 1960, Suburba built nine more
elementary schools, a middle school, and a high school. In the
1960s, three new elementary schools were built, four were expanded, a second middle school was built, and an addition was put
on the high school, including more classrooms, an industrial arts
wing, and a larger gym.

Today, more than half of Suburba's classrooms are at least
twenty-five years old, and some are close to forty years old. Even
though they have been well maintained over the years, they are
simply worn out.

The heating systems, for example, are not energy-efficient. According to a study conducted by the Greater Suburba Power Co. at
the request of the Suburba School Board, heating costs for at least

(continued)

Figure 3-2 *(continued)*

half of Suburba's schools could be cut by between 25 percent and 33 percent, and for another quarter of the schools by up to 15 percent, if modern heating equipment and better insulation were installed. In total, the power company estimated annual savings of between $125,000 and $145,000 if the modernization was completed.

What's more, several of the oldest elementary schools are literally falling apart. For example at Lincoln School, on West Main Street, which was built in 1948, settling has created several large cracks in the foundation....

                          # # #

in all future rides sponsored by the club must wear safety helmets, you might also issue an accompanying release giving National Safety Council or government figures on the number of head injuries suffered by bicyclists not wearing helmets.

You have to understand that some, perhaps even most, of the information included in a background news release may not end up in the story. If much or all of it does, great! But the real purpose of the backgrounder is to help put the overall story in perspective for the reporter, to underscore how or why it is important and why it therefore deserves more and better coverage. While the press of deadlines and competing stories may mean that the initial treatment of your story is cursory and seems to completely ignore the background information you provided, on more than one occasion I have seen a reporter or TV station come back days or even weeks later and do a longer, more in-depth piece inspired by the backgrounder.

3. *The feature.* Features are a kind of a catch-all category in that the length, style, and approach can vary greatly. As opposed to backgrounders, feature stories are usually more people-oriented and tend to be either more dramatic or more humorous in approach. More often than not, they are written in a lighter or more entertaining style. A sample of a feature story approach can be seen in Figure 3-3.

Feature stories often include profiles of people. You'd certainly want to profile each of the candidates for the beauty contest your local civic group is sponsoring as part of the county fair.

It's more than likely the media would be interested in a profile

Figure 3-3. Sample of a feature news release.

FROM: Consolidated Press Works
John J. Jones, Vice President Marketing
1234 Industrial Blvd.
Metrocity, California
Bus. 919 / 555-8888
Res. 919 / 555-7654

CONSOLIDATED'S ROOTS AS A "TINKERER"

Today's Consolidated Press Works, headquartered in Metrocity, Calif., traces its roots back over a hundred years to a one-man printing shop that specialized in "tinkering."

Today, Consolidated employs over 500, including 300 in its main manufacturing facility in Metrocity, another 150 in a warehouse and parts distribution center near Los Angeles, and approximately 25 each in sales and service offices in Europe and Taiwan.

That early one-man shop was started by Eldon Wilson, a Civil War Veteran, who, like so many of his contemporaries in the early 1870s, left the war-weary East for opportunities in the West. Wilson worked at various odd jobs in Kansas, South Dakota, Wyoming, and Nevada before coming to Metrocity in 1874. He landed a job with an early Metrocity weekly that eventually went broke.

Tired of moving around, Wilson took the defunct newspaper's dilapidated press in lieu of back pay and opened his own print shop. A self-described "tinkerer" with machinery, he soon had the old press running smoothly—and, in fact, developed several innovations that allowed the press to work more quickly and to produce print of higher quality than most presses of the day.

Word of his innovative concepts spread and soon he was making adaptations on presses all over the West. He received his first order for a complete new press in 1879 from a weekly in San Francisco....

# # #

of a man who's about to retire after forty years as a guard at your bank or of a driver who's just completed a million accident-free miles at the wheel of a semi for your trucking company.

Profiles can include nonhuman critters as well. A local museum got a lot of media mileage with a lengthy and detailed make-believe "profile" of its new mascot, a baby dinosaur.

Features thrive on human drama and conflict. Is your new controller a single mother who worked her way through college and graduate school while holding down a full-time job and raising two children? Did several dozen of your union members devote a weekend to rebuilding the home of one of their fellow members after it had been heavily damaged by fire?

Nostalgia pieces and local history are also staples of features. Was the founder of your agency or group a particularly colorful figure? In cleaning out some old files, did you discover a treasure trove of faded and crinkled, but still recognizable, photos dating from the early, horse-and-buggy days of your business?

At times the line between what's a backgrounder and what's a feature can be pretty vague. No matter. What's important is that you appreciate that there are differences—albeit sometimes subtle—between the two and that you start to keep a sharp eye out for story ideas about your business, agency, or group, regardless of which category they fall into.

4. *The follow-up.* This is the news release issued "for the record." It's usually sent out soon—very soon!—after an event to tell how much money was raised or who the new officers or board members are or how many people attended the concert or to report that a new membership goal was reached or that it was a good sales year for your business. An example of a follow-up release is seen in Figure 3-4.

Follow-ups can also be used to achieve "closure" on some controversial issue. For instance, say you get sued by some disgruntled employee you had to let go. When the initial suit is filed, the media very likely will jump all over it. However, when, after a year of hearings, motions, countermotions, and negotiations, you finally settle the dispute with the employee, you should then issue a follow-up news release outlining the major points of the settlement and laying the issue to rest.

THE IMPORTANCE OF A MEDIA KIT

What's a media kit? A media kit is one or more stories about your business or organization or agency, usually including photos, that is available on request to the media and other interested parties. Should you have one? Absolutely!

Figure 3-4.   Sample of a follow-up news release.

FROM: Have-A-Heart Workshop
        Ellen Gooding, Admin. Asst.
        407 County Building
        Franklin, Maine
        Off. 555-6789 Home 555-0987

FOR IMMEDIATE RELEASE

HAVE-A-HEART ELECTS OFFICERS

Mrs. Richard O'Roark of Franklin was elected president of the Have-A-Heart Workshop's Board of Directors at the group's annual meeting held Sept. 3. Mrs. O'Roark has been a board member for six years, previously serving as chairman of the Finance Committee, as treasurer for two terms, and most recently as first vice president. She succeeds Mark Taylor of Jefferson, who retired from the board after eight years.

Ray Brown, also of Franklin, was elected first vice president. In his third year on the board . . .

#   #   #

Big corporations usually have very impressive media kits, containing a half dozen or more professionally written articles (features and backgrounders about their products, their management, their position in the industry, their history), technical fact sheets, and 8 × 10 glossy black and white or color photos, all wrapped up in a slick folder or envelope. Yours may not contain much more than a sheet or two of information on your letterhead, but you should have one nonetheless. Appendix A shows the contents of a sample media kit.

Here's the minimum that you should have in your media kit:

• A narrative description of your current business, services, or products—in other words, who you are. It should especially include anything that makes you unique in your field—a specialty niche you serve, an exclusive brand or product you own or have developed, the geographic area you cover, a position of leadership in the industry. . . .

- A history of your business, group, or agency—in other words, how you got to be who you are, when the organization was established, why it was started, by whom, what it's accomplished over the years, how it's changed. . . .
- Brief biographical summaries of your founders, current management and board members, volunteer leadership—in other words, the people who count.

Optional extras might include:

- More detailed and/or technical information about your products or services.
- Product photographs.
- Head-and-shoulders photos of your management, board, or volunteer leadership.
- Reprints of articles about your business, agency, or group that have appeared in other publications.

Developing a Media Kit

When you're developing a media kit, the first place to look for help is your national trade association and/or your product suppliers or manufacturers. These people often have preprepared news releases and backgrounders and even photos available for the asking. You can use their prewritten material as is or take parts and add your own local material.

If you don't feel confident about writing your own media kit, get a local free-lance writer to help you. Ask your media representative for a name; chances are he'll know a reporter who does some moonlighting. Or call your local writers club or college.

Depending on how complex your situation is, a basic media kit with a photo or two can be put together for as little as a few hundred dollars. While this might seem like a lot, look at it this way: Just one good-sized story in a local paper or one guest appearance on a public service show would probably cost you that much or more if you'd bought an equivalent amount of ad space!

And, unlike an ad, which after running in the paper or over the air is gone, a media kit can be used again and again to generate stories in various kinds of media.

How to Use a Media Kit

Here are some typical situations in which you'll find a media kit useful, perhaps even the key element that gets you more publicity than you would have had otherwise:

• Your fifty-year-old retail shop has just been named the Small Business of the Year by the local chamber of commerce and a newspaper reporter wants to do a feature on you and is looking for background information. This is when those old-time photos of your grandfather in his general store in the early 1900s that you retrieved from the attic, along with some of his letters and account books that tell humorous anecdotes about being "paid" for groceries with fresh eggs or cut firewood, will become invaluable.

• Your high-tech electronics firm is about to announce the development of a new laser-based surgical instrument. Of course you'll develop a news release on the new instrument to send to all the trade journals, but why not include a full media kit about your business and the previous breakthrough discoveries you've made? The feature articles that may be generated could go a long way toward establishing your image as an industry innovator among customers or potential customers.

• Your small community hospital has just received a major federal grant to build a large new wing and position itself as a regional treatment center for cancer patients. Naturally you'll hold a full-scale news conference to announce this major new development, perhaps even inviting media representatives from a 50- or 60-mile radius. Every reporter who covers your news conference should get a media kit that not only details all the pertinent information about the new cancer wing but talks about the commitment to excellence in health care that has been the hallmark of the hospital for decades.

In other words, media kits are handed out at news conferences, are sent to the media—including nonlocal media—in connection with major announcements, and are used to respond to requests for information from the media.

But media kits aren't only for the media. They can be excellent sales tools as well. For instance, when attending a major trade show, why not take a supply of your media kits along? Certainly you'll pass out lots of business cards and perhaps even lots of copies of your basic brochure to just about anyone who slows down in front of your booth. But what if someone actually stops and talks for awhile, shows genuine interest in your products or services, and asks you to "send me more information"? Wouldn't it be a neat move to whip out your media kit at this point and say, "Listen, we just got our media kit updated for this show. Why don't you take one? It has most of the information you're interested in."

That potential customer is suddenly going to feel very complimented, as if you've done him a special favor because you're giving him something that's normally reserved for the media! That potential customer is certainly going to read everything in your kit—which is more than can be said for a lot of the so-called sales brochures I've seen—and is most certainly going to remember who you are and be in a favorable mood when you make your follow-up call later.

Getting Started Tomorrow Morning

At the end of the last chapter, I suggested that you review the list of fifty news release topics in the context of your business, agency, or group and jot down as many story ideas as occurred to you. Now go back over that list, asking yourself about each one:

- Is this news release idea best handled as an advance?
- Is it more suited to treatment as a backgrounder?
- Does this idea lend itself to feature story treatment?
- Is the story a more or less routine follow-up?

Again, don't worry if you're not sure where the line is that differentiates one kind of news release from another. There is no right or wrong answer here. Rather, this is just an exercise to get you used to looking for potential story ideas and to thinking in terms of what approach or treatment seems best.

4

The News Release: How to Write a Good One

In its simplest form, a news release is really nothing more than a statement of facts. When sitting down to prepare a news release, you should not get hung up on the so-called journalism style. Most of us are not Ernest Hemingway—who, it is said, was the ultimate master of the clipped, action-oriented writing style favored by journalists—and the media don't expect us to be. Remember, virtually all media rewrite whatever you submit to them to fit their own needs for style, length, or time anyway.

Rather, you should be more concerned with making sure that all the facts are there! A left-out key fact is far more likely to get your news release tossed in the round file than not being quite on target with the correct newspaper or electronic media jargon. Unless you're very familiar with and comfortable writing journalese, you're far better off with a straight fact sheet—a series of statements that cover all the essential information—than you are with a muddled attempt at being journalistic that only ends up getting in the way of the information. In fact, if your news release ends up sounding a little "Dick and Jane-ish," don't worry about it; you're probably OK.

THE TEN COMMANDMENTS FOR A GOOD NEWS RELEASE

While you needn't be overly concerned about the correctness of your writing style, you do need to know that there are certain rules as to how news releases should be structured or formatted that are absolute and inviolate. To ignore these will virtually guarantee a one-way trip to the round file for your material.

The ten commandments for structuring a standard news release are:

1. *News releases should be typed, double-spaced.* Never submit a handwritten news release. Period! If you don't type, find someone who does. Also, use nice, wide margins—at least an inch and a half, perhaps more—on both sides and at the top and bottom of your paper. Indent paragraphs five spaces.

These preliminary rules, along with several that follow, are designed basically to make the work of editors, news directors, and reporters a little easier. They all wade through a tremendous amount of data every day, making virtually instantaneous decisions about whether or not to use material, and if they do use it, about how to play it. The harder you make it for them to do their work—like forcing them to decipher a handwritten release—the more likely it is that your material will get short shrift or no shrift at all.

2. *The name and address of the business or group sending the news release should be prominently displayed at the outset.* Using your letterhead will normally suffice.

Editors and news directors want to know right from the start the source of the material they have received. Is it from a local source or from out of town? Is it a well-respected company or agency or some Johnny-come-lately they've never heard of? The fact is, the source of the material being submitted can have a significant impact both on whether an item is used and on how it is used.

3. *Always include the name and phone number of a specific person to be contacted for more information.* This is usually given with the identification of the source at the beginning of the news release, but it can be added at the end as well. But it *must* be included!

Be sure to include *both* a phone number where the contact person can be reached during the day (business) and a number where that person can be contacted after hours (home). For a couple of reasons. First, offering only a business number sends a not so subtle message to the media that your information really isn't very important, since you only want them to call you at your convenience. Second, if you think about it, most media people do much of their work in the evening—television reporters getting ready for the late evening news, newspaper reporters working on the next morning's edition—so it only makes sense to be available to the media when they are doing their work.

Unfortunately, this important piece of information is frequently left out. In most cases, the media want to talk to the contact person to get a routine fact clarified or to get some additional piece of information. But sometimes it's to arrange a photograph or a more in-depth interview or feature story. No contact name or phone number means a missed opportunity for more publicity!

By the way, be sure your contact person knows he or she might be getting media calls, is thoroughly familiar with the content of the release, and has the authority to make further statements or release more information.

4. *Include a release date and time.* Since most press releases are not that time-sensitive, you can usually use a standard phrase like RELEASE AT WILL or RELEASE AT CONVENIENCE, which simply tells the media they can use it whenever it's convenient.

Why at the media's convenience? Why not put a specific release date on everything? Because if, in fact, it doesn't make that much difference whether your material gets published tomorrow or the next day or even the day after that, then why tell the media it *must* be released on a specific date? If you do so, you run the risk of bumping up against some more important late-breaking news story and ending up with two paragraphs buried next to the hog markets. If you'd left it to the media's discretion, they might have held the story over until tomorrow, a lighter news day, so that you'd end up with more ink or airtime!

If, however, your material *is* truly time-sensitive, then use a *specific* date and time, like FOR RELEASE APRIL 3, 1990 or FOR RELEASE AFTER 5 P.M., CDT, MAY 24, 1989.

Never use just the day of the week—how will the editor know which Monday?—and always be sure to specify A.M or P.M.

Most media will respect your specified release date and time, and if they feel they can't for some reason, they will normally call to say so.

5. *At the top of your story put a suggested headline.* For example, if your release is about plans to add some new office and warehouse space to your present facilities, the suggested headline

on the main announcement story might read WIDGET MANUFAC-
TURING PLANS MAJOR ADDITION. A backgrounder accompanying the announcement that talks about the company's long roots
in the community might read WIDGET STARTED HERE AS BLACK-
SMITH SHOP A CENTURY AGO.

In other words, the suggested headline is always a brief statement of the most important or vital fact of the story. You'll rarely,
if ever, see the exact wording of your headline used in print.
Rather, it's there to give the editor or reporter a quick idea of what
the story is about.

6. *Always make your lead, or first, paragraph the most important item in the article.* Unlike a good joke, you never save the best
until last in a news release. The lead is the "sales hook" for the
editor and the reader alike, and should always be a logical extension of the suggested headline.

For example, the lead paragraph for the suggested announcement headline—WIDGET MANUFACTURING PLANS MAJOR AD-
DITION—might read: "Widget Manufacturing Co., of Hometown,
today announced plans to build a $1.5 million, 25,000-square-foot
office and warehouse addition to their present facilities at 123 Industrial Road."

7. *Follow up with the facts of your story in descending order of
importance.* In journalism schools this is always illustrated by the
use of an inverted pyramid, with the wide part at the top and the
point at the bottom. It's almost the exact opposite of how you're
taught to write in English composition class in high school or college.

The reason for this dates back to the old "hot type" days when
stories were set in columns of metal type. As the editor wrestled
to make things fit on a given page—sort of like working a jigsaw
puzzle with parts whose shape can be changed—he might pull a
story off the page and quite literally saw off the last two or three
paragraphs to make room for something else. Yet, because of the
tradition that the key facts come first, he could still be confident
that the reader would at least be getting the most important information in that now truncated story.

8. *If the main text does go on to another page, write MORE or
CONTINUED at the bottom of the page to indicate that this is not
the end.*

Then put a key word from your suggested headline at the top of the next page followed by the page number. In journalism jargon this is called a "slugline." For the story about Widget's expansion, the slugline might read WIDGET / PAGE 2.

You need to "slug" each page so that if the pages get separated they can be reassembled in the proper order. If you've ever seen the typical reporter's desk just before deadline, you'll understand why this is necessary!

9. *At the end of the main text of the article, signal that it is the end by putting in three pound signs, "# # #," the word "END," or the traditional "− 30 −."*

10. *After the end signals, put any special additional information that doesn't fit elsewhere.* This might include:

- The schedule for a special photo opportunity and/or interview availability.
- The date, time, and place of a news conference or site visitation.
- Instructions on how to get to the news conference site.
- Information on how to obtain media credentials.

Figure 4-1 is an example of a standard news release structure, in which the numbers in brackets correspond to the Ten Commandments just given.

THE FAMOUS FIVE W'S

Probably one out of three news releases submitted by nonprofessionals has one of the all-important Five W's either left out entirely or left incomplete. Check and then double-check your news releases to make sure all information is complete and clear. As I suggested earlier, incomplete or inaccurate information is a surefire way to get your news release quickly crumpled up and used for basketball practice into the nearest trash barrel—and make no mistake about it, most newsrooms have very large trash barrels!

WHO—Who's sending the release? Who's sponsoring the event? Who's the star attraction? Who are the new officers, the award winners, or the nominees? Who can attend? Who is the event for the benefit of? Who can be contacted for more info?

Figure 4-1. Example of a standard news release structure.

For: Quad Cities Regional Chapter,
      American Marketing Association [2]

FROM: David F. Ramacitti & Associates [3]
       319 / 323-7338

FOR RELEASE AT CONVENIENCE [4]

MIDWEST LIVING PUBLISHER TO APPEAR [5]

[1][6] Tom Benson, Des Moines, publisher of the phenome-nally successful *Midwest Living* magazine, will speak to the Quad-Cities Regional Chapter of the American Marketing Association, Thursday, April 13, at the Outing Club, 2109 Brady St., Davenport, Iowa.

[7] The meeting is open to the public, and professionals in marketing from all fields are particularly invited to attend.
MORE [8]

[page 2 of release]

BENSON /Page 2 [8]

A cocktail hour (cash bar) begins at 6 P.M., with the program starting at 7. A $4.50 charge will be collected at the door for hors d'oeuvres.

Benson will speak on "Defining a Midwest Life-style" and will discuss the market research involved in developing the profile of Midwesterners' attitudes and interests that formed the basis for the magazine's editorial approach.

Midwest Living is published by the Des Moines, Iowa-based Meredith Corp., which also publishes *Better Homes and Gardens* and *Good Housekeeping.*
[9]

[10] *ADVISORY TO MEDIA:* While *no* formal news conference is planned, Mr. Benson will arrive at the Outing Club at about 5:30 P.M., Thursday, April 13, and will be available for interviews.

FOR MORE INFORMATION: [3]
Dave Ramacitti
David F. Ramacitti & Associates
617 Brady St.
Davenpot, Ia 52803
Off. 319 / 323-7338; Res. 319 / xxx-xxxx

Always use full names, followed by an address or at least a home city. Never assume that the editor or the reader will know who you are talking about.

WHAT—What is it? Concert? Anniversary? Grand opening? Dance? Speech? Cleanup day? Award ceremony? VIP visit? Regular or special meeting? Expansion? Name change? New product or service introduction? Retirement or new hire?

In other words, give full information about what's going on, what's happening, what the story is all about.

If a schedule of events or activities is lengthy, such as for a festival that stretches over several days, then summarize the major activities in the general news release and include a full schedule on a separate sheet.

WHERE—Always use specific addresses for local events; never assume that everyone knows where even major facilities are located. "At the Civic Center" isn't enough. The reader may or may not know that the Civic Center is somewhere downtown. "At the Civic Center, 500 Main St." is the right way.

Add the city and state for out-of-town events or if you're sending your release to nonlocal media. If you ask the reader to write for tickets or other information, always include the ZIP code.

WHEN—This is probably the "W" that's most frequently left out or incomplete. For example, it's common for a news release to announce that a dance is scheduled for "Saturday from 8 to midnight," but then fail to specify *which* Saturday! Always use specific dates, *never* just a day of the week. Use specific dates for past events as well.

WHY—Why is the event happening? Is it a fund-raiser? A news conference for the purpose of making a major announcement? Why is it important to the community or the group? Is it a major award for the business or the first time something is being offered in this area?

The "why of it" is probably the second most frequently omitted or incomplete "W" and may be the most crucial one!

Editors and news directors daily make dozens of virtually instantaneous decisions about what they believe their readers need to know, which can be translated as what they understand their readers *want* to know. Make no mistake about it, whether they're conscious of it or not, editors and news directors are "marketing" their product, the daily newspaper or the 6 o'clock news.

The more you help them to "market" their paper or show by making absolutely clear *why* the information you're sending out will be of interest to their readers or viewers, the more likely you are to get a good play!

Finally, *HOW*—How much will it cost? How does one get tickets? How do people find parking?

My old managing editor used to insist, sometimes very loudly, "Never leave an unanswered question in the reader's mind!" It's a good rule to follow!

WHO SHOULD GET YOUR NEWS RELEASE?

In most cases, it's best simply to address your news release to a job title—Managing Editor for the print media, News Director for the electronic media—rather than to an individual by name.

Use individual names only if you're absolutely sure that specific person handles your material and is, in fact, still on the staff. Media people are notorious job jumpers, so the reporter or editor who was so helpful to you last month may now be at a desk a thousand miles away. No, your release will probably not be forwarded to that now-absent staffer, but it may float around the newsroom for awhile until it finds a proper home.

Also, be very judicious about sending multiple copies of your release to the same medium—for instance, one copy to the City Editor, a second copy to the Society Editor, a third to the Community Calendar Editor, and so on. If in doubt, don't! Here's why.

In most cases, the duplication will be discovered and only one will get used anyway, but the duplication will be remembered, and, like the fable in which the little boy cried wolf once too often, all of your next batch may be ignored by everyone! Or, worse yet, if there is a slipup, your release may run twice in the paper, which is embarrassing and will certainly be remembered, not fondly!

If you do send multiple copies to the same medium, then clearly note who all got copies on the release.

Exclusives and Scoops

Now, for the other side of that same coin. Be very, *very* careful about providing information to only one medium to the exclusion of all others. In journalism there is a very nasty thing called being "scooped." It means someone else had a news item you didn't. No one in the media likes to be scooped.

If a reporter or editor thinks you were responsible for his or her being scooped, that is, you provided some important story or piece of information exclusively to another, competing, medium, it most certainly will not be forgotten and will very likely have an unfavorable impact on how future items you submit are treated. So think not twice, but three, four, or more times before giving someone an exclusive.

However, there is nothing wrong with providing various news angles on the same story to different media so that each one will have a unique element to feature in its coverage. But you must be certain that the different angles you provide are of roughly equal news value.

For instance, to continue with the example of Widget Manufacturing's expansion, all media would get the basic announcement news release detailing how much the addition will cost, how many square feet are involved, when construction will start, who's building it, how long it will take, what kinds of new equipment it will house, and how many new jobs the expansion will create.

Going beyond these basics, you might then arrange with the local newspaper to do an accompanying background story that features old-time photos and anecdotes about how Widget has changed over the years since it was founded in the 1890s.

You might provide one TV station with a videotape showing how an automated parts warehousing system that will be used in the new facility works. This could be provided by the vendor of the system you're buying.

For another TV station you might arrange a special demonstration of how you've teamed up with the local community college to provide in-shop training for several existing employees, as well as some new hires, on operating a new computer-based order system you plan to install with the building expansion.

For a radio station you might arrange a brief interview with an employee who's been with Widget Manufacturing for over forty years and who could talk about the reorientation to high tech.

As you're discussing these specific story ideas with the individual media representatives, you should briefly outline the angles the other media representatives are going to take. You don't want anybody to be surprised by what's on another medium.

DEADLINES AND OTHER MATTERS

When should you send in your news release? For routine notices of upcoming activities, not more than fourteen or less than five working days prior to the event. For major events, at least thirty days and up to four months in advance of the event. For follow-ups, not more than two days after the event.

Should you send second notices and/or do phone call reminders? Yes, but judiciously. There definitely *is* a line that separates being helpful (by reminding the media of an important event) from being a pest. Unfortunately, there are no rules in this area, so you'll have to use your best judgment and play it by ear.

What are the "working" deadlines of the various media? Daily newspapers need to have a news release *in hand* not later than 9 A.M. for that day's afternoon edition; not later than 7 P.M. of the previous evening for the morning paper; and not later than the previous Wednesday morning for the following Sunday's feature section.

Most daily newspapers you will deal with will have either a morning or an evening edition, though a few will have both. Some of the largest urban dailies may have three or even four editions a day. If you are dealing with one of these, check on their specific deadline schedules.

Weekly newspapers need to have copy in hand no less than seventy-two hours (three working days) prior to home delivery. In other words, if the paper is received by most people in Thursday's mail, the deadline is Monday morning.

For TV news operations, the working deadline is usually three hours prior to their major early evening or late evening newscast.

For radio stations, the deadline is normally sixty minutes prior to their scheduled newscast.

Understand that most media have a number of deadlines. The preferred deadline for most media would be even earlier than these working deadlines. There is, of course, the absolute latest deadline, which means that only news of the magnitude of a presidential resignation or a confirmed landing by aliens from another planet has a chance of getting used at that hour!

How should your news releases be delivered? Practically all, or 99.1 percent, should be delivered by mail; .8 percent can be delivered by hand, but only by appointment; and .1 percent should be delivered by telephone or by hand without an appointment, but only in the case of emergencies!

In today's high-tech world there are lots of new delivery options popping up all the time. Yes, some sophisticated media may have modems or fax machines and can handle this form of instant delivery. But for ninety-nine percent of the news releases you'll be providing them, using a fax machine would be overkill.

ABOUT PHOTOGRAPHS

Most media prefer and even insist on taking their own photographs and/or videotapes. There are two good reasons for this:

First, if they take the picture, it means that they can control the content—the number of subjects and how they are posed or arranged.

While the presentation of a large check may be a big deal to your group, the truth is that a check presentation photo—with five, six, or more people all standing stiffly at attention, grinning stupidly at the camera, and holding some unidentifiable slip of paper—is incredibly boring from a media standpoint. In fact, most TV stations and many newspapers simply do not take check presentation pictures under any circumstances.

Second, and perhaps even more important, they can control the lighting and other technical elements to assure good-quality reproduction.

You're the rare exception if you or some member of your organization can produce professional-quality photo prints. In ninety-nine cases out of a hundred, the do-it-yourself photos you offer to the media will be rejected.

This is especially true of Polaroids and most "candid" color prints you take. These types of photos do not reproduce well in black and white; almost invariably they come out as dark blobs virtually without detail.

Getting Started Tomorrow Morning

Select one of the story ideas you came up with about your group, agency, or business and write down all the facts you can think of that are pertinent to that story. At this point, don't worry about writing in complete sentences or even about what order they're in. Just get down as many of the facts as you can.

After you've gotten all the facts down, go back over them and check them against the famous Five W's: who, what, where, when, and why. Are any of the Five W's missing or incomplete?

Go back over the facts again and this time ask yourself which is the most important fact. Why will your story be important or of interest to the reader/viewer? Have you made absolutely clear to everyone the gee whiz factor in your article?

Now reorder the facts, starting with what you have determined is the most important fact from the viewpoint of the reader/viewer and allowing the other facts to flow logically from that starting point.

Congratulations, you now have the rough draft of your first news release!

5

The News Conference

Presidents Kennedy and Reagan (when he held one) elevated the news conference to a high art. They always seemed totally in control in front of the media. Even when they didn't actually answer the question put to them—Kennedy was a master at using humor to deflect questions he didn't want to deal with—they were able to leave the impression that they had answered it.

Most likely, you'll never have to face high-powered national network correspondents like Mike Wallace or Sam Donaldson. But there may very well be occasions when you will want to—or must—hold a news conference for your business or organization.

Indeed, if the news release is the basic building block of an effective public relations program, then, by stretching the analogy a bit, I might say that the news conference is the decorative cupola on the roof.

Over the years the formal news conference has tended to be staged mainly for and identified with the electronic media. But if you have one, never forget to invite the print media people as well.

WHY AND WHEN TO CALL A NEWS CONFERENCE

The specific reasons you might have for calling a news conference closely parallel the reasons you'd have for sending out a news release, as covered in Chapter 2. A news conference is a far more powerful publicity tool than a news release. In the media's view it suggests something important and, therefore, tends to demand their attention. Which is why, a little like the boy who cried wolf too often, you don't want to call frequent news conferences for routine announcements.

There are several factors you will have to weigh and balance against each other in determining whether to call a full-scale news conference or just to send out a routine news release. One factor has to do with how necessary you feel it is for all the media to get precisely the same information at the same time.

For example, the announcement that your small, neighborhood shopping center merchant's association will be holding its annual sidewalk sale over the first weekend in May probably is best handled by a fairly routine news release. However, if the shopping center is about to change its name, undergo a complete renovation, and get a couple of major new tenants and plans to aggressively promote for business outside its immediate neighborhood, this certainly demands calling a news conference.

Availability of the news source or spokesperson is another factor. For instance, if the international president of Rotary is going to be the guest of honor at the fiftieth anniversary of your local chapter's founding and will be in town for only a few hours, then you might schedule a news conference just before the luncheon or dinner so that the media can interview your guest.

Yet another factor has to do with the magnitude of what you want to say. Let's take a look at something that happens regularly to most businesses and groups—promotions of personnel. The fact that you've promoted a shop foreman to a shift manager at your manufacturing plant, a counter clerk to an assistant buyer at your department store, a youth counselor to a cottage supervisor at your residential youth center, or an associate to a partner of your law firm, while certainly deserving of note, probably does not justify calling a news conference.

On the other hand, if the newly named CEO of your major local manufacturing plant represents the third generation to head up the family firm, or if the former head of the residential youth center was fired due to some controversy and the new director you're about to bring in is coming with lots of professional credentials—in other words, if there are some unique circumstances involved in your personnel change—then a news conference may well be warranted.

Last—and related to the magnitude of your message—is whether the size of your market warrants a news conference. An announcement that you're going to build a 25,000-square-foot office addition to your business and add between fifteen and twenty new jobs probably wouldn't be considered major news in a large urban market like Chicago or even Kansas City. So you would probably cover this announcement by a news release, distributed by mail, perhaps accompanied by a media kit that included a backgrounder or two and one or more drawings of what the new building will look like.

However, if this same business is located in one of the hundreds of medium-size to small towns across the country, say an area of 50,000 or under, then you probably should stage a full-blown news conference to make the announcement, complete with officials from the company, leaders from the local chamber and city hall, with comments from representatives of each, along with a media kit and easel-mounted drawings—or better yet, a model—of your new addition!

Here are a few rules of thumb for calling a news conference:

1. To make any major announcement ("major" being relative to your size and the size of your market), such as an expansion of your business, a new program or service offered by your agency, a new CEO....
2. To cover a grand opening or ground breaking.
3. To celebrate any noteworthy milestone, like the 100,000th customer or a fiftieth anniversary.
4. To tell your side of a controversy.
5. To show off a "big name" visitor.

How often can you or should you call a news conference? As with why, it's all relative. Unless you are unusually aggressive and resourceful, for *most* small businesses, agencies, or organizations, once a year might be a lot.

Conversely, if you are in an unusual situation, for instance, if you run a high-tech business in which major innovations are occurring almost daily, or you're an agency that's involved on the cutting edge of some important social or health issue, then two or three news conferences a year might not be out of the ordinary. And if you're running for political office or are in the middle of some raging controversy, weekly or even daily news conferences might well be needed.

THE TEN SECRETS OF A SUCCESSFUL NEWS CONFERENCE

As with the news release, there are certain do's and don'ts involved in holding a successful news conference.

1. *First and foremost, make sure your spokesperson is well prepared!* Write no more than a one-page statement—typed in ALL CAPITAL LETTERS, double-spaced, and with ample margins—for the spokesperson to "read" to the media (I'll have more to say about "reading" later). When read at a deliberate speed, this formal statement should not take more than sixty to seventy-five seconds.

The statement should be a brief summation of the most important information being announced—not necessarily *all* the information being announced. This formal statement is basically designed to give the electronic media a brief clip they can put on the air. It is not the place to go into tedious background detail.

Be sure to have copies of the statement to hand out to reporters at the news conference.

In addition to this formal statement, you should prepare three to five "talking points" that are brief, one-sentence summaries of what you want the public to remember about the subject of the news conference. These are the points the spokesperson will stress again and again when answering questions from the media.

Remember, the TV and radio folks will be looking for what they call fifteen-second sound bites to put on the air. Keep your sentences simple and declarative. "KISS" is an old axiom in journalism; it stands for "Keep it simple, stupid!"

2. *Have your spokesperson rehearse several times,* ideally in front of someone's home video camera so that he (or she) can actually see himself on TV via a VCR playback, to polish up his presentation. If a video camera and playback aren't available, then at least have your spokesperson rehearse in front of a mirror.

The ideal is for your spokesperson to look directly into the camera as if he were speaking face-to-face with just *one* viewer out there. Unfortunately, for those not used to the lights and cameras, the experience can be horribly intimidating. An acceptable alternative to looking directly into the camera is to look slightly off camera, as if the spokesperson were talking to a reporter who had just asked a question.

"Reading" a statement is somewhat more complicated than it sounds, because while you can and should appear to be "reading" the statement, you must not be dependent on it. As a spokesperson, it's OK to have a statement in front of you, and it's OK to glance at it occasionally. But it's definitely not OK to have your eyes constantly downcast while reading the statement in a nervous monotone.

While you or your spokesperson may, in fact, be a pillar of integrity to the people who know you off camera, to the viewer out there a spokesperson stumbling around on camera, eyes shifting nervously from the statement to the camera to somewhere off camera, gives every appearance of being incompetent if not downright untrustworthy.

3. *Offer something visual other than a "talking head."* This is the somewhat derisive term the electronic media people have for a close-up shot of someone talking into a camera. I can't emphasize it enough: TV reporters hate talking heads! Having something visual besides a talking head significantly increases your chances of getting a spot—or a longer spot—on the early or late evening news.

If you're going to build a new building, for instance, place several architect's renderings of the exterior and interior near the spokesperson on easels. After the spokesperson has made his statement and the reporters have asked their follow-up questions, I virtually guarantee that one or more of the TV crews will take numerous close-ups of the drawings and that these visual images will dominate the on-the-air report.

If you're adding a new product, have someone demonstrate it. Or ask the manufacturer to supply you with videotape clips of the product in use.

If you're announcing an upcoming event, like a festival, stage a brief activity that would be typical of the festival, or, at minimum, provide slides from last year's festival.

4. *Be sensitive to what's going on behind your spokesperson.* A plain background, such as a curtained wall or even the sky, is ideal. What you don't want is a lot of distracting activity or "busy"

decoration competing with your spokesperson. What you don't want is a tree growing out of the spokesperson's head or a lot of idiotic camera hogs mouthing "Hi Mom" in the background.

5. *Always have a media kit ready to be handed out.* If your spokesperson's statement is going to be limited to one typewritten page, as I've suggested, then how do you provide all the rest of the necessary background information to tell your story? With your media kit, of course.

The media kit should include a copy of the statement to be attributed to the spokesperson and, in addition, one or more background articles, biographic or historic data, fact sheets, even technical product information if needed.

Distribute copies of the full media kit to those who didn't make it to the news conference immediately after the conference, either in person or by mail.

6. *If possible, schedule your news conference for mid-morning, between 9 and 10:30 A.M., so that the afternoon papers can use it.* An afternoon news conference means that the electronic media can get something on the air that evening, twelve or more hours ahead of the newspaper's morning edition the next day. In the competitive media world, that's no way to make friends with the print media.

Mondays, Thursdays, and Fridays tend to be the slowest news days during the week, so schedule your news conference for one of these if you can. Avoid Tuesdays and Wednesdays, which are the days after most city council and school board meetings and tend to generate more "important" breaking news, and weekends, when there are only skeleton reporter and/or camera crews on duty at most media.

7. *After the formal part of the news conference is over, try to give the media a chance for a brief one-on-one interview with your spokesperson.*

The electronic media like this because it gives them a chance to show their reporter on camera with the spokesperson. This is especially true if your spokesperson is a "big name," such as an entertainer or sports figure.

The print media like the one-on-one question because it gives them a chance to come up with an "angle" to their story that will vary slightly from that used by the electronic media.

8. *Announce your news conference in such a way as to maximize attendance.* You want to give the media enough information to pique their curiosity, but not so much that they can run a bare-bones story and skip the news conference.

Emergency situations excepted, try to give the media four or five working days notice of your scheduled news conference; two working days is the minimum for an advance-planned news conference.

Notify them by mail with what's often referred to as a media advisory, an example of which is seen in Figure 5-1. In format it's virtually identical to a news release, except that it gives the time, place, and reason for the news conference. Should you follow up with a phone call reminder on the day of the news conference? Yes, but keep in mind my previous caution about bugging the media.

Here are some tricks for getting the media to show up at a news conference:

- Tease them with some gee whiz material that clearly illustrates the importance of what they're going to hear, but does not give away the story. Let them know why you are having the news conference—say, to make a major announcement about your business and new jobs—but don't provide any details, such as how big your expansion will be or how many jobs you'll create.

- Let them know you will have visual materials available other than a talking head—tape clips or slides for the TV people, photographs or drawings for the print media.

- Say there will be time for questions and answers with whoever is making the announcement, because it's through this format that individual reporters are able to get something unique to feature in their reports.

- Let them know they will have access to someone with authority. In the minds of the media, a spokesperson is often viewed as a lackey. If they understand they will have access to an acknowledged expert or authority, a recognizable name, the CEO, or a top government official, they are more likely to show up.

Figure 5-1.   Sample advisory to the media announcing the holding of a news conference.

FROM: Dwight R. Smith, Vice President Marketing
        S&J Manufacturing Co.
        Factorytown, Ill.
        333 / 654-3210

NEWS CONFERENCE ADVISORY

S&J TO ANNOUNCE EXPANSION PLANS

S&J Manufacturing Co., 5874 Old State Route 2, Factorytown, Ill., will hold a news conference at its plant site at 10 A.M., Monday, March 3, 1989.

The news conference is being held to announce plans for a major building expansion at S&J, and the opening up of new jobs.

The news conference will be held in the first floor conference room of the S&J headquarters building, immediately to the left as you enter the plant's main gate off Old State Route 2, and will be followed by ground-breaking ceremonies at the expansion site.

Attending will be:

- U.S. Senator G. W. Grimes, who assisted S&J in securing a Small Business Administration loan to help build the new addition.

- Mayor Anne C. Carmichael of Factorytown, who will present Factorytown's Outstanding Citizen Award to Frederick R. Smith, founder of S&J.

- Frederick R. Smith, 91, who, with his partner, the late H. L. Jorgenson, founded S&J Manufacturing in Factorytown in 1938. Mr. Smith will use an S&J-manufactured front-end loader to turn the first bucketful of dirt to start construction.

- Frederick R. Smith, Jr., son of the founder and currently chairman and CEO of S&J. Mr. Smith will unveil a scale model of the new addition and will announce details of the expansion and talk about its impact on Factorytown.

Following the news conference, buses will be available to take guests, including the media, on a tour of the S&J facility and to the site of the expansion for the ground breaking.

#   #   #

MORE INFO: Dwight R. Smith
             Vice President Marketing

S&J Manufacturing Co.
5874 Old State Route 2
Factorytown, Illinois
Off. 333 / 654-3210
Res. 333 / 654-8881

Most media will play fair and come to the news conference—where they will get the information at the same time as everyone else. But every once in a while, you'll get a reporter who'll try to wangle things out of you in the hope of getting a jump on the competition. The reporter will claim the paper is short-staffed due to vacations and ask you to give all the details right now, over the phone.

If you know the reporter who is asking this favor and *if* you feel you can trust him and *if* you're sufficiently knowledgeable of his deadline situation so that you're sure that by talking to the reporter now you won't give him an unfair jump on everyone else, then go ahead and do an over-the-phone interview.

However, if a reporter asks for a phone interview after the news conference—perhaps requesting that someone read the statement over the phone—don't hesitate to cooperate to the fullest degree possible.

9. *Have the news conference room already set up and ready for the media's convenience.* Make sure it's big enough to handle a minimum of a dozen people in a smaller market and two or three dozen in a medium to larger market. This almost automatically dictates the use of a large conference room and eliminates most offices.

If possible, avoid outdoor news conferences. Even on nice days the elements can still cause problems of wind, lighting, or blowing dust. If a site visit would add value to whatever it is you're announcing, then hold the formal news conference indoors, followed by a media tour of the site.

Virtually empty the room, or at least the major center portion, of furniture—tables, chairs, large conference tables, and so on. Place chairs for reporters and guests to sit on and tables for handouts, coffee, and refreshments at the back of the room, behind where the cameras will be.

Always provide a speaker's lectern. First of all, the speaker will need a convenient place to put his or her notes. Even more important, having a lectern to hold on to will also help alleviate the all too natural nervousness an inexperienced speaker feels facing a battery of cameras and reporters.

If there are models, products, drawings, plans, charts and graphs, or other objects important to what's being talked about, then place these at the front of the room, either on a table or easels immediately adjacent to the speaker or mounted on the wall to one side of the speaker.

Make sure there are plenty of power plugs for the electronic media—one wall plug simply won't make it! If you have to, run heavy duty extension cords from other rooms.

Since most rooms you will use will be rectangular rather than square, set up the room lengthwise instead of crosswise. In other words, place your lectern and tables or easels against one of the wide walls, with the media facing the lectern. Why this way? For one reason, all the media like to be in the front row of the press section. Allowing a very wide first row may make a second row unnecessary. For another, it's better for your speaker. The farther apart the media can place their bright lights, the better, both because it reduces the harshness of the shadows on the speaker's face and because it helps keep the lights from shining directly in the speaker's eyes, which always tends to produce a squinty, nervous look.

10. *Finally, feed 'em.* Yep, put on the coffeepot and put out a plate of donuts and sweet rolls. No, it won't get you a banner headline for a routine story, but it will be appreciated and remembered. *Never* serve liquor at a news conference. This is a working situation for the reporters and cameramen; liquor is inappropriate.

Getting Started Tomorrow Morning

A news conference is something like a stage performance, with image playing as key a role in its success as the content of what's announced or discussed. You wouldn't go on stage without having practiced your lines; neither should you hold a news conference without having practiced. Here are a couple of ways you can get some of that practice.

Hold a mock news conference. If you have a friend with a video camera, fine. If not, perhaps a local community college or technical school with a communications lab could be induced to cooperate in what would be a learning experience for its students. Prepare and deliver your statement to the camera, hand out media kits, and have friends or students pretend they're reporters and ask you follow-up questions. At this point, don't worry so much about *what* you say, but be sensitive to *how* you say it. Study the playback several times. Are you at ease? Do you look as if you're in control? Do you seem genuinely excited about what you're announcing?

Develop a brief program about your business, agency, or organization and make presentations to school or church groups, business or service clubs, retiree groups, just about anyone who'll listen. As you develop your speaking skills in front of these usually friendly and hospitable groups, the idea of facing a battery of TV cameras and a bunch of reporters throwing questions at you should become less intimidating. Speaking before groups also forces you to see yourself as others see you, and, depending on the kinds of questions that these audiences ask, can give you a fairly good feel for what kinds of questions reporters are likely to come up with.

6

Newspapers:
The Backbone of
Your Publicity Program

In recent years many daily and weekly newspapers—like all the mass media—have experienced something of a decline in their traditional dominance of local markets. Even so, the hometown paper remains today, and probably will continue to be for the forseeable future, the backbone of the public relations program for most small businesses, professional firms, service agencies, or volunteer groups. There are several reasons why this is the case:

First, the local community newspaper is still by far the most accessible of all the mass media in terms of your being able to get editorial coverage on a regular basis, particularly of so-called routine news.

Second, especially when you factor in this "free" news space, the newspaper is still one of the least expensive ways of reaching a significant number of people with your message.

Third, newspapers are information-intensive: They *want* to know what your business or group is up to. Reporters and editors are fact freaks and data junkies. The writers who are considered the "best" in the field are those who can pack the most information into the least amount of space.

Finally, newspapers are still the single most universal medium. That is, most people still take and faithfully read their hometown daily or weekly paper.

MAKING NEWSPAPER TRADITIONS WORK FOR YOU

The fact is, the traditional roots of the newspaper as an institution are very much in your favor. Newspapers started out as just that, *news*papers. Television and radio, by contrast, from their very inception have been entertainment-oriented.

America's founding fathers believed that a broad diversity of locally owned and edited newspapers was an essential element in a democratic system, providing for a free—in the sense of open and uncensored—exchange of ideas and information. This is why for almost 200 years the U.S. Postal Service had a subsidy built into the postal rate structure for "real" newspapers, although that subsidy was phased out in the early 1980s.

Whether daily or otherwise, a newspaper, both by tradition and regulation, must have a majority of paid subscribers in order to qualify for special postal rates and priority treatment as a newspaper, to be recognized by various industry-sponsored circulation auditing groups, and to be accepted by the community it serves as a "real" newspaper.

This is one of the newspaper's major strengths. Because it is a by-choice purchase by the reader, each purchase is, whether consciously or not, a vote of confidence by that reader. There are lots of free-circulation publications similar to newspapers, and these certainly should not be ignored in your media planning, but a paid circulation base is, and probably will continue to be, the industry standard.

Most newspapers, whether daily or weekly, define their market base in terms of geography. Think about that, because it's an important point! It is a fundamental assumption of most newspapers that they serve the information needs of a given community, metropolitan area, or rural area. And that they must, to some degree, serve *all* their readers in that area. In other words, they must be *all things to all people!*

The point is, the local newspaper, by tradition, tends to think of itself as the community's official diary keeper. That's why newspapers have historically incorporated such titles as news, times, register, mirror, or record. Your small business or volunteer group can very likely benefit from the local paper's tradition as the com-

munity's "newspaper of record" and get increased coverage simply
by asking for it.

THE VARIETY OF NEWSPAPERS TO CHOOSE FROM

There are almost 8,000 nondaily newspapers published in the
United States. Most are published weekly, some twice weekly,
some biweekly, and some only monthly. Nondaily newspapers pre-
dominate in:

- Small communities and/or rural areas where there is not
  enough circulation or advertising base—let alone news—to
  support a daily paper. They almost always specialize in local
  community and county news and rarely publish state or
  national news.
- Suburban areas, usually surviving under the umbrella of a
  larger, dominant daily from an adjacent central city. The
  suburban nondaily survives by providing more local news
  and advertising for the specific community it serves than
  the big daily can. These papers also tend to ignore state or
  national news.
- Specifically defined market niches, for example, an ethnic
  neighborhood or some sort of special interest group (this
  kind of publication is discussed more thoroughly in Chapter 9).

There are nearly 2,000 daily newspapers published in the
United States. Daily newspapers also come in a wide variety of
types and styles.

Some are published five days a week, Monday through Friday,
usually in the late afternoon. These tend to be found in smaller,
stand-alone cities with populations between 15,000 and 35,000, or
they serve one or more suburbs of about that size. In fact, many of
the original suburban weeklies first established in the 1950s and
'60s around megapopulation centers like Los Angeles have themselves grown up to be dailies.

Some are published six days a week (add Saturday morning),
but this is a dying breed.

The industry standard for most daily newspapers is to publish seven days a week in the morning. In fact, the trend is decidedly toward morning papers, with many evening-only papers switching to morning and many papers that once published two editions a day "going morning."

Only in the very largest urban areas, like New York, Chicago, or Los Angeles, do dailies publish multiple editions throughout the day, called by varying names such as "street edition," "home edition," "metro edition," "state edition," and so on.

As a rule of thumb, you can figure that the more local a newspaper is to you, the more likely you are to get some or even lots of coverage of your business, events, or activities. And, conversely, the more distant a newspaper is either in terms of geography or size, the less likely you are to get some or any coverage. In other words, the small-town weekly or the small-city daily that serves your community is far more likely to publish your business brief about an employee you've promoted than is a large urban daily. In fact, the larger urban dailies should probably be categorized with the national networks as basically inaccessible to the small business, agency, or volunteer group for whom this book is written.

HOW NEWSPAPERS ARE STRUCTURED

A key element in getting your fair share of coverage from your newspaper is understanding how newspapers are structured. On weekdays most daily newspapers regularly have:

- A front news section reserved for world, national, state, and very important local news.
- A local news section with the more routine, day-to-day material.
- A features, life-styles, or entertainment section, which can vary greatly in the amount of local material it carries.
- A sports section.
- Individual pages (sometimes sections) devoted to business and stock market news, people news (or what used to be known as "society" news), and editorials and letters.
- Perhaps one special section, dedicated, say, to food and rec-

ipes on Wednesdays, when the food ads run, or a weekend activities and entertainment section on Thursdays or Fridays.

On Sundays many daily newspapers may also have:

- A home section, featuring house plans, fix-up ideas, recipes, decorating and gardening tips, and other how-to material.
- A travel and leisure section.
- An arts, music, and book review section.
- An expanded editorial or issues section.
- An expanded business or financial section.
- Special interest sections that vary with the season.

Nondaily papers don't have nearly so formal a structure as dailies do, but they do have some:

- Page one is reserved for the most important local news.
- A page or series of pages will normally be devoted to other, more routine local news.
- A page or series of pages may be devoted to feature articles, or to people news and/or society items (weddings, engagements, anniversaries).
- There's usually an editorial and letters page.
- Sometimes there's a sports page (or pages).
- And, like the dailies, they also tend to publish an occasional special section devoted to a specific topic—for instance, a devastating hurricane or a centennial or bicentennial celebration.

Newspaper people like to talk about "hard" and "soft" news. Hard news, of course, takes in the plane crashes and earthquakes, the political shenanigans and the stock market vagaries, the city council debates and the school board discussions. ... Hard news is still the staple diet of the newspaper, and it is the arena in which your news release will generally compete for space and/or airtime. That's why much of this book focuses on preparing your media materials and developing your contacts in the so-called hard news arena.

When newspaper people talk about soft news, they are usually referring to feature stories and personality profiles, weddings and engagements, movie and book reviews, calendars of community events, and articles on places to go and things to do. And they mean the special sections—the bridal tab, the lawn and garden section, the spring home repair section, the auto repair section, the home buyer's guide, the travel planner, the special section marking the anniversary of some community institution, or the community progress report usually published near the beginning of the new year.

Special Sections: A Great Opportunity

Even though editorial people—reporters and editors—sometimes look down on the special sections, the fact is that special sections offer excellent opportunities for small businesses to reach targeted potential customer groups with free editorial exposure.

More often than not, these sections are designed primarily as advertising vehicles, that is, to provide a self-contained package on a given subject—gardening, boating, home improvement, electronic gadgets, fall yard work, winter recreation—in which the advertiser is guaranteed that the adjacent editorial material will complement his ad message.

Usually the editorial copy used in these sections is generic material provided at no cost by a national trade association, a public relations firm or ad agency on behalf of one or more manufacturers, one of the wire services, or one of the various feature article syndicates that newspapers belong to. It's generic in the sense that it usually does not mention specific brand names and almost never has any specific local flavor.

Most of the time this editorial material is simply rewritten by a copy editor at the local newspaper to fill up the holes around the ads. Few, if any, changes are made, except in length. However, every once in a while the newspaper will make an effort to localize the material, to see if there is some unique angle or aspect that would make the material more interesting and useful to local readers.

This is where your diligence in studying the paper and in building contacts with the right editors or reporters can pay off.

Perhaps you've noticed that the paper has published a special section in the past on a topic related to your business. Perhaps you've written a letter or two complimenting it on this section, but, at the same time, pointing out some unique local angle, which, if it had been included, would have made the special section much more useful to the paper's readers. Perhaps you've even made an appointment with the reporter or copy editor who handles this material. And you've carefully cultivated this relationship and perhaps even established yourself with this reporter or editor as the local expert on this particular topic. So the next time the paper does a special section on this topic, they turn to you for the local angle.

Who Makes the Decisions

Not only should you be aware of how daily newspapers are structured in terms of where they put things, it is also important to understand how they are structured in terms of who makes what decisions. The publisher is *the* boss. He or she is the CEO of the newspaper. However, except on the smallest of papers, the publisher usually has very little to do with the day-to-day news operation, that is, with whether your news conference gets covered or where your news release is played. About the only time the publisher gets involved in the "news side" is when the paper endorses a political candidate or takes a stand on a controversial issue.

This isn't true in all cases, however. On some papers, especially if the person carries the dual title of editor and publisher, the publisher may, indeed, get very heavily involved in the news side.

Similarly, the editor—also sometimes known as the editor-in-chief—rarely gets involved in the nuts-and-bolts operations of the newsroom. The editor is more involved with administering the news department, like dealing with budgets and personnel problems, and with handling overall policy matters.

It is the managing editor—also known by such names as executive editor, metro editor, deputy editor, associate editor, and news editor—who wields the real day-to-day power in the newsroom. It is the managing editor who usually has the final say about which news conference will get covered and which one skipped, which story gets the banner headline and which one gets relegated to the hog markets page.

Depending on the size of the newsroom operation, there can be varying levels of what are often referred to as subeditors working under the managing editor, including:

- A city editor, who is normally responsible for seeing that news from the urban area, like city hall, the police department, the courthouse, the school board, is covered.
- A state or regional editor, who takes care of news items from the outlying areas.
- A wire editor, who stays on top of national and international material coming in over the "wire" (now by satellite).
- A features editor, who takes care of things like people stories, society news, movie reviews, the TV log, comics, and the community calendar.
- An editorial page editor, who drafts or writes editorials and edits letters to the editor and syndicated columns.
- Several copy editors, who assist with writing headlines, checking spelling and punctuation, and dummying pages in many areas.

These jobs are fairly standard. That is, you'll find these folks at most papers regardless of size. Larger papers, of course, will likely have many more editors for specialized areas—the arts, entertainment, business, education, science, the outdoors, agriculture. . . .

Finally, there are the reporters. On most newspapers there are two kinds of reporters: general assignment reporters, which means that they can be assigned to virtually any story, to wherever they are needed most at a particular moment; and "beat" reporters. A beat in newspaper jargon means a specific area a reporter is assigned to cover, such as city hall, the county courthouse, the schools, the police department. . . .

On some of the largest dailies, you'll perhaps run across a reporter who bills himself or herself as an investigative reporter. Investigative reporters became the rage after the Watergate scandal. The irony is, true investigative reporters would just as soon not be so visible about their status lest the sources of the inside information on which they thrive dry up through fear of being traced.

While the lowly reporter might appear to be at the bottom end of the organization table, the truth is that on many papers experienced reporters are given a lot of freedom to generate and pursue article ideas on their own.

It is neither practical nor necessary for you to get to know the publisher, the editor-in-chief, the managing editor, and every subeditor and copy editor on a first-name basis. At the same time, it is important to watch the paper to see if one reporter's byline consistently pops up in a field you're interested in. If you're a small business, do they have a full-fledged business editor, or at least a reporter who specializes in business news? If you're a hospital or health-care professional, do they have a reporter who specializes in health stories? If you're a bed and breakfast facility, is there a travel editor, or perhaps one reporter who does most of the travel writing? If you're a school administrator, do they have an education writer?

An important fact of life in the newspaper business is that a story idea generated by an insider, a reporter or editor, has a greater chance of getting good play than a story idea generated by an outsider, such as in a news release. So, even if you don't quite reach the ideal status of becoming the newspaper's chief expert on a specific topic, developing a friendly relationship with the right staff member can still keep the channels open for you to "plant" a story idea now and again.

SEVEN STRENGTHS YOU CAN BUILD ON

When putting together your publicity programs, here are some of the strengths of newspapers you can build on:

1. *The newspaper is still a good way, possibly the best way, to reach the largest share of the community.* The fact is, most people—perhaps up to nine out of ten homes in smaller communities, and as many as six out of ten households in larger

areas—still take and regularly read their local daily or weekly paper.

2. *The newspaper reaches a broad spectrum of the community,* most age groups, most occupation groups, most neighborhoods.

3. *The newspaper is an information medium.* That is, people come to it with the primary expectation of receiving information on some topic of interest to them. The electronic media, by contrast, tend to be seen primarily as entertainment vehicles.

4. *The newspaper is your medium of choice if the message you're trying to get across is information-intensive,* for example, your position on some complex issue.

5. With its tradition of being the community's diary, *the newspaper is by far the easiest medium of all in which to get some kind of coverage,* even of routine material.

6. *The hometown newspaper tends to have a high level of believability in the minds of most readers.* If they see it in the paper, they tend to take what is said at face value and to believe it is the truth.

7. Although you do have to be aware of deadlines and other basic rules, *the newspaper doesn't require a lot of lead time,* especially by comparison with other media.

SEVEN WEAKNESSES

As is often the case, many of the newspaper's strengths can also become its weaknesses. Keep your expectations realistic by watching out for:

1. *The shotgun effect.* Because newspapers go to a cross section of the community, you may not always reach the groups you especially want to or need to reach.

2. *The one-shot syndrome.* Newspapers rarely repeat announcements, so you only get one shot at getting your message out. If for some reason people missed the story in yesterday's pa-

per, well, you know what they say about nothing being as stale as yesterday's news.

3. *The lack of control over how your material is edited.* "They sure chopped that story up!" is the perennial complaint of PR people, professional or otherwise. Copy editors will often shorten, rearrange, rewrite, sometimes even combine your news release with other material to the point where it barely resembles what you sent in!

4. *Having no control over how and where your material is presented.* Some days you may get a multicolumn headline and six or eight inches of space on the front of the local news section, while other days you'll be lucky to get a one-column headline in microscopic type buried on the legal notices page.

5. *Being always at the mercy of breaking news events.* Hopefully, you won't ever be unlucky enough to schedule your news conference to show off plans for a new addition to your store or factory at the same time the President decides to announce a major breakthrough in disarmament negotiations with the Soviets!

6. *Poor reproduction, especially of photographs.* Although improvements are always being made in press and prepress technology—just look at *USA Today*—newspapers are still the poor relations when it comes to first-class reproduction. If good reproduction is essential to getting your message across, for example, that your beauty salon has just won a national hairstyling competition, the newspaper would not be a good place to try to visually portray the subtleties of your winning designs.

7. *A short life span and relatively poor pass-along readership.* Unlike magazines, which people tend to keep around and read several times, then pass along to friends, relatives, or the beauty shop or nursing home, most newspaper readers will read the paper tonight and take it out with tomorrow's trash.

WHAT NEWSPAPERS WILL AND WON'T USE

Another key to getting your fair share of newspaper coverage is to have a pretty good idea of the kinds of things they are likely to say yes to and of what they'll probably reject. Newspapers, by tradition, will generally use most items that are "for the record," such as:

- Personnel changes, like elections of officers, promotions, retirements, new management.
- Announcements of events or activities, like club meetings, open houses, dances, seminars, lectures, fund-raisers, flea markets, church bazaars.
- Results of activities, for example, how much money was raised or how many people attended or, in the case of businesses, the dollar volume or percentage increase of a special sale.
- Milestones, like awards, anniversaries, or recognitions, a typical example being a real estate broker who has joined the Million Dollar Club.

Newspapers like *local issue backgrounders.* Unfortunately, most businesses tend to treat anything even remotely resembling controversy like the plague. Yet there is often opportunity for excellent positive exposure if the issue is approached correctly.

One way might be to offer some insights on how local people could be affected by a nonlocal problem or issue; you don't necessarily have to take sides on the issue to talk about the local impact. For instance, a local commodities broker might issue a statement on how a pending railroad strike could affect local farmers.

Another approach is to provide some special background on a nonlocal issue. How many times have you seen people quoted because they once served in a current overseas hot spot in the Peace Corps or did a stint there for their company?

Finally, on a hot local issue many newspapers would be glad to cooperate if you helped to arrange guest editorials offering both the pros and cons of the issue. Naturally, you would be one of the guest editorial writers.

Newspapers love *local feature stories.* Here the sky's the limit. The opportunities are bounded only by your imagination:

People helping people is a surefire angle. A case in point: Some vandals damaged the front of City Hall and a local contractor volunteered to clean up the mess. It may have cost him a day or two of a crew's time and materials, but he got a page one photo in the local newspaper and film on two of the three local TV stations. That's positive exposure no amount of money can buy!

People in conflict will almost always pique an editor's curiosity. The best kind of conflict situation is where the "little guy" wins over the "big guy," especially if the big guy is the government or a large, out-of-town corporation. Did you land a contract in competition with a "bigee"? There might be a story for the business page in how you did it.

Success stories are virtually guaranteed to get you some coverage, especially the classic rags-to-riches variety. The story can be about your company—how it grew from nothing to ten employees and $2 million in sales in just thirty-six months—or it can be about one of your people—the high school dropout, for instance, who joined your warehouse crew three years ago, went on to get his high school equivalency, and associate degree, and is now programming your computer system.

Personality profiles are to newspapers what desserts are to diners! The more colorful, unique, or innovative, the better. Do you have an employee who dresses up as Santa and visits children's hospitals at Christmastime? Is there someone in your shop who's come up with a revolutionary new money-saving or quality-enhancing wrinkle to your manufacturing process?

Finally, newspapers like *anecdotes and local history.* Anecdotes are generally humorous and are usually good items for the local gossip or society column. There is nothing wrong with your business getting mentioned in a positive, even if humorous, context in a local column. In fact, in many communities getting a mention in one of these columns is something of a status symbol.

If your business has been around awhile, say fifty or more years, there may well be some old photos, maybe even some diaries or letters, dating back to those early years that would make a good feature story, especially in connection with your anniversary.

And here's a list of what most newspapers will not consider:

- Photos of check presentations (in the trade they're known as "grab'n'grin" shots; does that tell you something?), ground-breaking and group photos of more than half a dozen people—beauty queen candidates excepted.

- Poetry, essays, and membership rosters.
- Events or announcements for members only, not for the general public.
- Old news—more than two days after the event.

The "News Curve"

Marketers are familiar with the so-called product curve, which basically tells us that different stages of a given product's life demand different promotional approaches. There's also a kind of "news curve," which tells us that a newspaper is *more* likely to print items that are short, timely, about recognizable people, very obviously local, not too controversial, of interest to a great many people, and have some gee whiz element to them.

A newspaper is *less* likely to use news items that are long, very controversial or sensitive in nature, of limited interest, highly technical or legalistic (translate that as dull!), not local, and not timely.

Getting Started Tomorrow Morning

Study your local newspaper. Look carefully at the different sections it has, at the section titles, at what day of the week they run, at what audience segment they're targeted—yes, even the good old "all things to all people" newspaper is trying to do some target marketing—at the particular topics that seem to be hot, at the sources of the articles (local staff writer? wire service? free lance?), and at the writing style used.

Make some notes of the things you notice. After a week or so, you may be surprised at the patterns that are emerging. You'll observe:

- How the paper is structured: where they tend to place certain types of news, how much space is given to various types of news, whether they use photos.
- What kinds of issues or topics they're following: Do national topics outweigh local issues? What kinds of local topics do they favor?
- Where local story ideas tend to come from: Are they mostly off

the wire? Do they seem mainly staff-generated? Or do they appear to emanate from some dominant organization, like the local chamber of commerce or some other group?
- Which local staffers regularly cover specific local topics.
- How they handle controversy, if at all.
- What their political viewpoint is.

As before, this is an exercise designed to increase your sensitivity to the specifics of your local newspaper or newspapers.

After studying the paper for a few weeks, you may want to pull out the list of story ideas you wrote for your business or group and see if what you've learned about the paper changes your ideas in any way or suggests some new ones.

7

TV and Radio:
The Media Darlings

Television and radio are the darlings of the media. They're so immediate, they're what's happening now! They're so universal that just about every town has at least one radio station of its own and virtually everyone watches TV at some point during the day. They seem to have an incomparable ability to influence how we feel about things, which is why politicians and McDonald's spend so much money on them. And they can create instant stars—just ask Vanna White!

FROM VAUDEVILLE TO VANNA

To truly understand the electronic media and how to use them effectively in your publicity planning, you have to understand their traditions. These are almost the diametric opposite of a newspaper's. Television and radio trace their roots to minstrel shows and vaudeville. In other words, they are essentially entertainment media. Just think about their recent history: radio of the 1930s and '40s, with its daytime Ma Perkins and Arthur Godfrey, evening Fibber McGee and the Green Hornet; television in the '70s and '80s, with its MTV and miniseries, HBO and Johnny Carson, Vanna White and Bill Cosby; and today's radio, with its "Wolfman" Jack and Bruce Williams.

This is a critical distinction that you must appreciate. What it suggests is that the typical consumer turns to television or radio with the basic expectation of being *entertained*—not informed or educated. Of course many choose to watch CNN and public broadcasting on television, or listen exclusively to news stations on the radio. But by any measurement standard I'm aware of, they are definitely in the minority.

The management of the news and/or public affairs departments in the electronic media are keenly aware of their strong traditions in the entertainment industry and, whether consciously or not, make judgments accordingly on what they will or won't use in their newscasts. Like it or not, the most successful electronic media publicity campaigns invariably have a strong undercurrent of show biz.

The degree to which you can find an element of entertainment in your news story and play it for all it's worth will very much influence the amount and frequency of coverage you can command from the electronic media.

No one, least of all the TV and radio news directors, expects you to trot out dancing bears or the Rockettes at every news conference. That sort of heavy-handed pandering to the cameras will usually backfire. If anything, it tends to draw attention away from—not toward—the important information you are trying to get across.

Rather, what I am suggesting here is simply that you be sensitive to the electronic media's unique ability to portray color, action, and sound and that you use those capabilities in your publicity programs. Remember how in Chapter 5 (on news conferences) I harped on having visuals for the electronic media such as drawings on easels, transparencies, tape clips, and even live demonstrations. These are simple examples of what I mean when I suggest adding an element of entertainment to your news conference. While dancing bears will probably end up competing with your information, carefully designed visual elements can enhance and reinforce the strength of the message you're trying to get across.

HOW THE ELECTRONIC MEDIA WORK

The typical local commercial television station has both a major early evening newscast and a late evening newscast. The industry norm for these programs is still thirty minutes, although some major markets have gone to sixty minutes. In addition to these major evening newscasts, there may be a thirty-minute news program during the noon hour, plus several five- to fifteen-minute news shows in the early morning or very late evening hours.

All electronic media have some form of public service programming. During the Reagan years, under somewhat more relaxed federal regulatory standards, some electronic media have been experimenting with less traditional approaches to public service programming. But for TV the norms are still:

- One or more thirty-minute talk, analysis, or public service show, featuring local guests and broadcast on a more or less regular weekly basis.
- PSAs (public service announcements) run in unsold ad slots, usually on behalf of a major national charitable organization or cause and normally featuring a name star or personality.
- Local community calendar announcements, sometimes sandwiched betwen shows in prime time but more often than not run during the late movie or on Sunday morning.
- In larger metro markets, locally produced telethons, sometimes strictly for a local cause but more often in conjunction with a national charitable group.

Public service programming norms for radio are:

- Five-minute newscasts just before or just after the hour, with perhaps a fifteen- or thirty-minute expanded newscast in the early morning, at noon, and in the early evening hours.
- PSAs and/or community calendar items at random times throughout the day.
- Five- to fifteen-minute prerecorded, interview-style featurettes that generally fall under some umbrella title like "Our Schools" or "The Chamber of Commerce at Work," usually broadcast at off hours, like the very early morning.
- Occasionally a "live remote" that may be tied in with a joint sponsorship of a fund-raising or other public service event, similar to TV's telethons.

Deadlines

Because they are so immediate, the electronic media are a good deal more flexible with respect to deadlines than are the print media. Indeed, they can change, add to, and/or update a news event as it's happening, even offer us live coverage of a major breaking story.

However, in that most of us don't deal in major breaking stories, it is almost certainly to our benefit in the long run to provide the electronic media with realistic lead times so they can plan accordingly:

For coverage of a news conference, the lead time should be at least two business days in advance, preferably four or five.

For PSAs, give both the TV and radio folks at least four weeks lead time before your event.

A guest shot on some local TV public service programs may be booked months in advance, especially during the fall and early winter seasons, so contacting the TV public service people as much as six months in advance isn't out of the question.

Who Makes the Decisions

While the print media tend to follow a fairly traditional, pyramidal organizational table when it comes to who decides what gets printed in the editorial columns, the electronic media, by contrast, tend to have a more diversified organizational structure that resembles a team more than it does a hierarchy:

The boss at most broadcast stations is the station manager or general manager. He or she is the CEO, the administrative head. Except for the most sensitive matters, he or she rarely gets involved in the day-to-day operations of the news or public affairs departments.

The news director is in charge of the newsroom operation. Like the editor-in-chief of a newspaper, he or she will probably be more concerned with administrative duties and broad policies than with details.

The assignment editor, on the other hand, is the one, as the name implies, who decides which events and/or stories the TV or radio news reporters will cover and when. For most small businesses, agencies, and volunteer organizations, the key person is the assignment editor.

At smaller radio stations the news director and assignment editor jobs may be combined.

Probably of equal importance to the do-it-yourself publicity practitioner seeking access to the airwaves is the director of community affairs (the title may vary). This person, though not usually part of the news department, does nevertheless work very closely with the news people, as well as with the programming people, to schedule public service programming and public service announcements.

On some larger-market TV or radio stations, there may be a feature or life-style reporter who's also worth getting to know. These people often enjoy considerable elbow room to generate their own story ideas, especially in the human interest area.

Finally, the radio or TV sales manager may also be a key player, since the idea for a "live remote" is often generated in the sales department, then worked through public service and/or news.

STRENGTHS AND WEAKNESSES OF TELEVISION

Television as a publicity medium has four unique strengths:

1. It can reach huge audiences on the national level. The Super Bowl, for instance, measures its audience in the tens of millions. It can even reach very substantial numbers at the local level because practically everyone watches at least some television every day, even if it's only the early or late evening news and the weather forecast.

2. TV has a tremendous potential for delivering a message with very high impact. Television combines sight, sound, action, and color. Just think what a profound impact on public opinion television news reports have had over the years—Martin Luther King being confronted by snarling police dogs in the 1960s, students protesting the Vietnam War in the 1970s, terrorists killing Americans in the 1980s. . . .

3. As a kind of corollary to the above, television is by far the best medium for conveying an image or emotional message. Think

about it for a second: A newspaper is essentially a word medium; readers have to supply the mental pictures through their own imaginations. By contrast, through using the right visual cues, television can communicate a powerful image message in seconds. Remember those haunting images of starving children in Ethiopia?

4. Finally, it is not too difficult to get *some* exposure for your events or activities—from public service announcements to guest shots on talk shows, from a telethon to a full-scale news conference.

Television's weaknesses include:

1. The shotgun effect. If most people watch some television every day, what this means is that you may indeed reach a lot of people with your message but this audience may not include the people you want or need to reach. For example, while your news conference to announce the opening of a new shelter for homeless people may, indeed, reach the community at large from whom you are expecting contributions, it will likely not reach many of the street people the shelter is designed to serve. In other words, with TV you have little, if any, audience control.

2. You only get one shot at it. Except for public service announcements, which may be run more than once, television virtually never repeats a story. When the TV people show up at your news conference or come out to cover your event, you have to be ready for them then and there. There's rarely a second chance.

3. As with newspapers, you have no control over what's said and how it's played; once you've staged your news conference or sent in your news release, it's out of your hands. The TV reporter can downplay or overplay your story; he can change the slant, combine it with other items, or dig up problems from the past. . . . And there isn't much you can do about it, except live with it.

4. It is very difficult to get any kind of coverage of routine and/or positive news on television. TV thrives on action, conflict, controversy, catastrophe. It tends to avoid talking heads that are saying nice things. There are a few minor signs that this attitude is changing, at least in some markets, but the progress is grudging and slow.

5. You are always at the mercy of breaking news, even at the local level. The news feature on your new expansion that the TV people said would run "at least a couple of minutes" may get chopped down to thirty seconds or bumped altogether because the mayor unexpectedly called a news conference to announce that a new business is coming to town.

6. While public service announcements are a wonderful opportunity for you to get some exposure for your group, always remember that a PSA runs because that time slot was *not* sold. This means that PSAs tend to be scheduled at off times, for instance in the middle of the late, late movie, when only insomniacs are watching.

STRENGTHS AND WEAKNESSES OF RADIO

Among the strengths of radio are:

1. It too can reach some fairly respectable audience numbers. These will certainly not be as high as TV's and probably not even as high as a well-read community paper's, but they can be large nonetheless. Most people listen to the radio at some time during the day, even if it's only in the car on the way to and from work. But then some folks listen to the radio all day long!

2. Of all of the mass media, radio at the local level offers the best potential for audience targeting. All radio stations try to establish a certain personality by targeting certain demographic groups. You'll often hear radio advertising salespeople talk about their station as being "number one for eighteen to thirty-year-old females" or as "dominating the morning drive time." By being aware of which station is targeting which group, you can to some degree target your message as well.

3. It's relatively easy to get some kind of exposure on radio. For one thing, radio tends to use more public service announcements than TV. It also has more frequent newscasts—usually every hour on the hour. Of course, there are the news/talk stations that are *always* looking for guests. There are live remotes and, if you're really lucky, you can get a disc jockey excited about what you're doing and end up with lots of plugs.

Radio's weaknesses include:

1. Again, the shotgun effect. You may not always be reaching the people you want to reach. If you're announcing a great new service that would appeal to mature people, what difference does it make if the local rock'n'roll station runs a bunch of PSAs for you?

2. You have little or no control over what is said and how. Even as a guest on a talk show, you can't always predict what kind of curveball question a faceless and nameless caller may throw at you (see Chapter 8).

3. The impact potential isn't very high for radio. Most people listen to the radio while doing something else, so they may not be really listening. Radio lacks the visual impact of TV. And there are the button punchers, the folks who jump from station to station, looking for their favorite song and/or avoiding news reports or commercials.

4. Like newspapers and TV, you're at the mercy of breaking news events.

5. Except on the news/talk stations, it is very difficult to get any kind of in-depth coverage on radio.

TURNING ON THE ELECTRONIC MEDIA FOLKS

Here are some hints on how to turn on a TV assignment editor:

• Above all, promise and deliver action and color. Again, TV hates talking heads. Analyze whatever it is you're trying to publicize and add activity and color, even if you have to stage it.
• Get to the point quickly and simply. Whether you're doing a formal news conference or making an appearance on a talk show, let the reporter or host know you have two or three simple and straightforward talking points you want to emphasize and reassure him you're not going to get bogged down in a lot of background stuff.
• Try for something original. Unique and/or first-time events in your community will generally get a positive response

from the TV people. But you have to make sure that the uniqueness is very clear and easy to see.
• Involve the public. Events or activities that are directed at and open to the general public will also usually get some kind of attention from TV.
• Make use of kids, dogs, and big names. Anytime you can *legitimately* involve one of these old standbys, you'll help your cause. And don't fall into the trap of thinking the big name has to be Robert Redford or Raquel Welch before you'll get some notice. You may snicker, but I know of a local business that got a ton of exposure on TV (and in the newspaper, too) by arranging an appearance of the original 1950s Lone Ranger.

Here's how to get the attention of radio assignment editors:

• Provide a sound opportunity other than a speaking human voice—music, sound effects, whatever. This is analogous to the action and color suggested for TV. For some really top-notch examples of how you can use just sound to create all kinds of images, listen to National Public Radio's daily news program "All Things Considered."
• Get to the point quickly and clearly. Electronic newspeople use the term "sound bite" to designate the recorded statement of a spokesperson. They *never* want a sound bite to last more than fifteen seconds!
• You'll especially attract the radio folks if you can assure them that you will offer a one-on-one chance for a sound bite with a big name.

TIPS ON HOW BUSINESSES CAN USE TV

First, if you send out a news release, don't just send it to the print media, assuming that it's too routine for TV to be interested in. Even if the TV news people do ignore your material, all that you've lost is a few cents in postage. And you never can tell when they might just decide to do a special series on local businesses doing innovative things and suddenly your routine news release becomes the nucleus of a two-minute feature aired on both the early and late evening newscasts.

Another way to generate TV coverage is simply to ask for it. For example, when a local hardware store has its annual manufacturers' representatives day in the spring, all the local TV stations are invited to prearranged individual interviews on the latest lawn-care techniques or demonstrations of gee whiz gardening gadgets. It's become sort of a local tradition that the TV stations kick off spring with a visit to this particular hardware store.

Yet another way to generate TV coverage for your business is, if they won't come to you, for you to go to them! A local hospital, using its own professional-quality video equipment and one of its own RNs, who's very good in front of a camera, produces and distributes to all the local TV stations two or three ninety-second health reports each week. At least one of the local stations routinely includes the report as part of its newscast. Of course, most small businesses don't have their own video equipment and couldn't afford to have it done by an outside agency on a routine basis. But maybe they could produce a five- to eight-minute sales video. And maybe, through some creative editing, three or four ninety-second minifeatures could be developed from the longer tape and simply given to the media for use at their convenience.

Provide file film that involves your business. I'll say it again, TV hates talking heads and loves visuals! Just to provide some visual relief from yet another shot of the anchorperson, a talking head, the producers will often flash up on the screen file film relating to the story being reported on: The city council OKs funds for a new fire station, so they flash up file film of a spectacular local fire.

Does your business lend itself to being used as file film? For example, are you a trucking company? Maybe you could provide file film of one of your trucks rolling down an interstate highway, perhaps with some shots of the driver inside the cab and maybe backing up to a dock. So that the next time they have a story about the trucking industry, it's your film—with a brief glimpse of your logo on the side of your truck as it passes by, as well as on the hat the driver is wearing—that they show.

Consider holding a media day. It's sort of like an open house, only strictly for the media—and, yes, you should invite spouses/

guests. You arrange special tours and demonstrations as well as interviews not only with the big wigs but with the frontline folks as well. A media day is more likely to work for a recreational or leisure-oriented business, such as a golf course, water slide, or resort, than it is for an accounting firm or a small manufacturer. And, it probably won't fly in larger urban markets, where media tend to shy away from this kind of thing. But in medium and smaller markets it's worth a try.

You might look into becoming an expert or analyst for one of the TV stations. In recent years, even TV stations in smaller markets have been turning more and more to local experts to provide some sort of "what does it mean to us" insight on a regional or even national issue. Subject areas for which these experts are most often sought include business and the economy, agriculture, politics, health, and technology. If you are a fairly well recognized expert in some specific area and are comfortable in front of people (and cameras), it's certainly worth your while to query whether any of the local stations are interested.

Try sponsoring a community event. Major corporations have discovered the value of sponsoring events, which is why there isn't a major national golf tournament that doesn't have a corporate sponsor. The same rationale, scaled down, of course, holds true for local businesses sponsoring local events. Bicycle shops can sponsor bicycle races or safety rodeos; sporting goods shops can sponsor Little League championship tournaments; manufacturers can sponsor a senior or special Olympics; a law firm can sponsor a high school invitational debate contest.

Give something away to a school or charitable group. Are you replacing your outdated personal computers with newer versions? Then why not give your old ones to a local high school to use in its computer classes? Even a worn-out old truck might still be useful to a community college or vocational school mechanics or body shop class. And you might get more mileage out of it by giving it away than by trading it in and sending it to the scrap heap.

Do something really unexpected or out of the ordinary for your business. For instance, if your store or shopping center has never stayed open all night for a special sale, then stay open around the clock, scheduling all sorts of entertainment and/or food throughout the night. The key to grabbing some TV time with this kind of event is to be "audacious," which Webster defines as being bold and daring.

Finally, a brief word about public service announcements (PSAs). While they are not available for profit business, they provide an excellent opportunity for nonprofit organizations and community groups to gain additional electronic media exposure. Local groups are most likely to get a PSA to help promote their specific events, such as an open house, fund-raising dance, rummage sale, workshop, or seminar. Usually PSAs are written by and scheduled through the electronic media's public affairs department rather than their news department. Most of the time the regular news release you send to the news department will get forwarded to public affairs if the news director decides not to do anything with it. However, sometimes it doesn't. So, it's a good idea to send a copy of your regular news release to both the news director and the community affairs department, of course noting on each that you've sent a copy to the other.

Getting Started Tomorrow Morning

As with newspapers, after studying this chapter you will probably see and hear TV/radio news from a wholly different perspective. Good!

Keep mental, if not written, notes about what you're seeing and hearing. Ask yourself:

- What kinds of local topics do the TV and radio newscasters tend to concentrate on?
- Do certain reporters have specific beats or topics they cover?
- How often, if ever, do they use feature stories about local small businesses, agencies, or groups? Why do they do them, what's the news angle?

About now some interesting patterns should start to become apparent:

First, you'll begin to notice that the two different media—print and electronic—tend to do certain types of stories exclusively. That is, you'll see things in the paper that you won't see on TV, and vice versa.

Second, there will be a few things—usually major news items—that both will cover, but usually from different angles or with a different emphasis.

Finally, they tend to play off of one another! You might see a feature on a unique new business in the newspaper one Sunday, only to see a profile of the same business pop up on one of the TV newscasts a week or two later. It works the other way too: Soon after a TV station begins a series on local schools, you may notice beefed-up coverage of the school board in the paper.

Once again, go back to the lists of story ideas you've made for your business, agency, or group. Can you now sharpen the focus of some of those ideas, that is, define more specifically what the story is about? Are you beginning to get a feel for which story ideas would work best on TV and which would go best in the newspaper? And do some new article ideas come to mind?

8

Talk! Talk! Talk!

Whether it's the middle of the morning, the middle of the afternoon, or the middle of the night . . . whether you're in Middlebury, Vermont, or Middle Amana, Iowa, or Middletown, California . . . turn on the radio and chances are good you'll pick up at least one news/talk station, and likely two or three.

With so many people doing all that talking, is anybody listening? You bet! What's more, the people who listen to all those TV and radio talk shows also talk about what they've heard to friends, relatives, neighbors, and colleagues at work.

If you want a well-balanced publicity program, don't ignore the local radio and/or TV talk show. If you do, you may be missing an opportunity to generate some very positive word-of-mouth exposure for your small business, agency, or group.

DIFFERENT KINDS OF TALK SHOWS

First, we need to differentiate among the various kinds of talk/interview shows that might be available on television or radio in your market.

As mentioned earlier, TV stations devote a certain portion of their airtime to public service programming. More often than not, this takes the form of one or more thirty-minute talk or interview shows each week. These usually consist of a living room-like setting in the TV studio, a regular host/interviewer who asks questions, and one or two guests who answer them.

In most cases, especially in small and medium-size markets,

these TV talk/interview shows don't deal with sensitive issues or get into controversy.

In the larger markets, however, in addition to the traditional thirty-minute public service shows, there may be one or more "real" talk shows that do get into some very weighty—though not necessarily controversial—topics. For many years, Irv Kupcinet, a columnist for the *Chicago Sun-Times*, had an after-midnight Saturday night talk show on a Chicago TV station that was a "must stop" for any literary or entertainment celebrity visiting the Windy City. And don't forget, Phil Donahue started out with just a local TV talk show in Dayton, Ohio!

These shows normally run from sixty to ninety minutes and have live studio audiences, which sometimes interact with the guest, as with Donahue.

Then there is the ubiquitous radio phone-in show. It is perhaps ironic that this type of talk show has acquired a reputation for stirring things up! The fact is, of the literally thousands of hours of airtime that are devoted each week to radio phone-in shows all across the country, only a relatively few of those hours actually deal with controversial topics or degenerate into shouting matches between guest and host or name-calling bouts between a guest and a phone-in listener.

Most of the time the guests are locals who are more or less well-known in the community. The host usually has asked the guests what they would like to talk about. And the phone-in questions are mostly cream puffs.

Many of these shows, whether on radio or TV, have a theme or specific subject that they deal with on a regular basis. Maybe one of the local TV station's thirty-minute public service shows is devoted to the schools. Perhaps one of the regular radio talk/phone-in shows only deals with sports. Possibly the local public broadcasting FM radio station or the educational TV channel will have an interview show featuring books and authors.

Regardless, almost all these shows have one thing in common—guests! Without a continuing stream of fresh and interesting faces for the host or studio audience or phone-in listener to relate to, there would be no talk show!

This is where you come in!

HOW TO GET TO BE A GUEST

Talk shows also have something else in common—a producer. The producer is the person who puts the show together—develops the topics or themes, puts together the calendar of future shows, searches out, interviews, and books guests, and makes arrangements for visuals.

Sometimes the host/interviewer is also the producer, though this is rare. Sometimes the station's director of public service or community affairs—the title varies—is also the producer, though this too is rare.

At all the larger stations, the producer will have a staff of assistants and researchers to handle most of the day-to-day details.

Becoming a guest on a talk show is easy—*if* you can just get the producer's attention. Unfortunately, getting the producer's attention is easier said than done. Lots of other people are trying for the same thing.

It's just common sense. The more popular a given talk show is—say one with the national impact of a Phil Donahue or Larry King—the more people who have axes to grind will vie for a guest appearance on that show—to promote their latest book, to hype their newest movie, to champion their favorite cause. Conversely, the more limited (translate that to read "local") a show is in its exposure, the less competition there will be for guest appearance slots.

Assuming that you are a small business, agency, or club that has neither the need for nor interest in being a guest on Donahue or the Oprah Winfrey Show, here are ten steps you can take to land a guest appearance on a *local* TV or radio talk show:

1. Consult the media contact file (see Chapter 11) you have been keeping to refresh yourself on exactly when the various talk shows in your market are broadcast and whether they revolve around a theme or topic.

2. Next, call the particular stations that carry these talk shows and ask who the producer is or who arranges for guest appearances.

If you are given two difference names—for instance, Mary Smith is the producer, but it is Joe Jones, her assistant, who books guests—address all correspondence to the producer, because that's where the decisions are made.

If the receptionist says, "That's Mary Smith. Just a moment, I'll put you through," smile and chalk one up for your side. And, of course, be ready to talk to Ms. Smith about your idea in detail.

More likely, you will simply be given a name. Fine, that's all you really have a right to expect at this point.

3. Now write a query letter to the producer in which you ask to appear as a guest on the talk show (see Figure 8-1 for a sample query letter). Make no mistake about it, this is a *sales* letter. It's up to you to *sell* your idea and yourself to that producer.

The letter itself should not exeed two single-spaced typewritten pages. It should summarize why you think you ought to make an appearance on the talk show, what you want to talk about, why you are qualified to talk about this subject, and, most important of all, why the show's audience would want to hear what you have to say!

I can't emphasize this last "why" enough, because it is mostly on the strength of the reasons you give that the producer will make his or her decision about booking you. Stress how what you have to say will have some important impact on the community.

For this purpose, you should review the suggestions given in Chapters 6 and 7 as to the kinds of things that excite newspaper editors and news directors. Many of these same things will help you to get the attention of a talk show producer as well.

If explaining all these "why's" is going to require more than two typewritten pages, then provide supplemental background or fact sheets, newspaper or magazine article clips, or whatever, but keep your letter to two pages!

4. Practice your presentation. More than likely you will be asked to come to the TV or radio station for a screening interview. What the producer will be trying to determine is not only whether you do, in fact, know what you're talking about, but also how well you talk about it. In other words, the studio people will be checking your "media presence," whether you're at ease in front of a

Figure 8-1.   Sample query letter written to the producer of a local public service show.

Mr. Ralph North, Producer
"Spotlight Suburba"
KSUB-TV Channel 9
P.O. Box 999
Suburba, Georgia 45678

September 5, 1989

Dear Mr. North:

First, let me thank you for giving me so much of your valuable time during our recent phone conversation and for encouraging me to write this query letter outlining our idea for an appearance on "Spotlight Suburba."

As I explained briefly over the phone, our recently established service business is called Thank You's To Go. We select, handwrite, address, and mail all sorts of greeting, birthday, thank you, and other types of cards or acknowledgments to the customers of our clients.

We believe a program about Thank You's To Go would be of interest to your viewers because it is a truly unique business.

First, the service is unique in our area, the nearest similar service we know of being more than 250 miles away.

Second, it is unique in how we operate it. My partner, Mary Alice Forester, and I, along with our receptionist, are the only full-time staff. We work with our clients to design a program of cards to be sent and develop the mailing lists, order the appropriate cards, distribute them to our associates, pick up the completed cards, and mail them. All our associates work in their own homes, at their own pace, at their own hours, and are paid on a piece basis. Our associates are about equally divided between young mothers of preschool children who want to work part-time and retirees. Surprisingly, among our retiree associates, there are slightly more men than women!

Third, we have enjoyed unexpected success in our first few months of operation. Our business plan was based on signing up one new client a month for the first eight to twelve months. In our fantasies we had hoped for two a month. But since starting four months ago, we have averaged four new clients a month.

Mary and I are members of the local National Association of Women Business Owners (NAWBO) and feel we are representative of a growing national trend of women entrepreneurs.

We have several dozen color slides we have taken of our associates working in their homes, and we would be glad to arrange a live demonstration in your studio. We also have several professionally done flip charts that Mary and I use in a presentation on women entrepreneurs, which we have given to several women's clubs and business groups.

In addition, you might be interested to know that our business was featured on the business page in the *Suburba Times* eight weeks ago and that the nationally circulated NAWBO monthly newspaper is planning an article on us in the next month or so.

We would be more than happy to arrange an interview at your studio at a time convenient to you to discuss our idea. Again, thank you for your interest. Our business number is 333–4321. My home number is 333–9876 and Mary's home number is 333-5432.

Sincerely,

Anita Anderson
432 West 3rd Ave.
Suburba, Georgia 45678

---

camera or microphone, whether you can state your case succinctly and in laymen's terms, whether you can evoke enthusiasm for your topic.

You don't, of course, have to be as smooth as Walter Cronkite to pass. But you do need to demonstrate some degree of being comfortable in the media limelight. If you're not used to being on camera, or even to speaking in front of groups, this could be a very tough assignment. There is only one way to develop that kind of easy presence—practice.

Practice what you're going to say in front of a mirror. Talk to any group that'll schedule you. Join a local club—such as the Toastmasters—or take a course—like a Dale Carnegie public speaking course or one offered by your community college—that forces you to speak in front of groups. Practice.

5. Establish your expertise. Remember, experts do not become so merely by virtue of academic credentials, although these certainly help. Someone who has kept house for thirty or forty years is more than qualified as an expert on homemaking. Someone who has bought and sold antiques for twenty-five years certainly qualifies as an expert on antiques. Someone who has just completed a 3,000-mile cross-country bike ride certainly qualifies as an expert on bicycle touring. Someone who has successfully operated a small business for two or three decades certainly qualifies as an expert on the problems of running a small business.

If you can establish your expertise on some topic, you may be surprised at how often you'll be asked to appear on radio and TV talk shows in your area, perhaps as part of a panel, a mix of local and out-of-town guests.

6. Be prepared to pinch-hit. Sometimes a scheduled guest will pull out at the last minute. If you've been able to establish that you're knowledgeable in a field of general interest and that you're reasonably articulate on the air, you may be the "volunteer" who is able to step in at a moment's notice. If you find yourself in that happy situation, then you're "owed one" by the show's producer.

7. Be sure your appearance is timely. Even in medium and smaller markets, the TV public service talk shows are often booked months in advance. So, if your appearance is to promote a specific upcoming event, such as a community festival or a major fund drive, be sure to contact the show's producer at the earliest possible moment in your planning cycle.

8. Try to latch on to hot topics. Every year some new issue or group of issues seems to spark the fancy of the media. These may be of national importance or strictly local. AIDS, drug abuse, entrepreneurs, afffordable child care, "wellness" and good health,

being competitive in world markets, and whether inflation is or is not under control are just a few of the hot topics that dominated the national media in the late 1980s.

Locally the media tend to reflect these national issues, but with some localized angles. Alternatively you could develop hot topics that are specific to your area. Should you pass a local option sales tax? Should your two hospitals merge into a regional medical center? Are your schools doing a good job? Are drugs a real problem among the young people of your town? Should you enact a "no growth" zoning policy in your community?

The likelihood of your being offered a guest shot on a talk show is directly proportional to how closely you can connect what you have to say with one of these national or local hot issues.

9. Illustrate your topic. The likelihood of your getting a "yes" out of the producer of a TV talk show is also directly proportional to the quality and quantity of your visuals—slides, videotapes, even live demonstrations. Either in your initial letter, or most certainly in your interview, emphasize that you have some exciting visual material available.

10. If all else fails, produce your own show. No, I don't mean that you should buy a half hour of TV time and say whatever you want to on the air, although this has been done more than once. What I'm suggesting here is that if you think you have a topic of demonstrable importance to the community, then line up a panel of potential guests (making no promises, of course), develop a series of discussion-provoking questions for the host to ask, and present your idea to the show's producer. If your topic has been well thought out and your proposed guest list is balanced, you might be surprised at how agreeable to your idea the producer will be.

This approach isn't going to work every time. But in some circumstances the resulting positive exposure you'll get may be well worth all the work of setting it up.

HOW TO HANDLE YOURSELF AS A GUEST

Now you've landed that coveted guest spot and you don't want to blow it. So here are ten more tips on how to handle yourself.

1. Most important of all, be prepared. As with news conferences, this is the key to success in handling yourself with the electronic media. Develop three or four talking points, one-sentence
summaries of the most important points you want to make during
your appearance. Memorize them. And work them into your discussion and into your answers to questions as frequently as
you can.

2. Be enthusiatic! I don't know how many times I've seen
people get on a talk show and suddenly turn as formal as a mor-
tician. They never crack a smile. They stare blankly at nothing.
They answer questions in one-word monotones. This kind of performance virtually guarantees that hundreds of viewers will grab
for the channel selector to find something more interesting.

Do you *really* care about the topic you're discussing? Then
show it. Wave your arms if you want to. Sit on the edge of your
chair. Smile and laugh. Believe me, no one will think you are silly.
Quite the contrary. Your friends and colleagues will tell you how
"wonderful" you were on TV, they'll say you "sure got your point
across," and they will marvel at how "relaxed" you looked.

3. Be conversational. It's another key to looking relaxed on
TV or sounding at ease on radio. Refer to your host by name. If
you need to address a phone-in caller, say "my friend."

On a talk show never, ever read from a prepared statement or
script. Even on radio, it ends up sounding stiff and formal. If you
want to quote something, quote it indirectly or paraphrase it.

4. On TV look at your host or at one of the other guests, but
never at the camera. There are two reasons for this:

One, if you look at the camera you're automatically going to
stiffen up, because for most of us a TV camera is still a very intimidating thing. So avoid the problem by pretending the camera isn't
there.

Two, pretending the camera's not there is the accepted con-
vention even among professionals on talk shows. When Buddy
Hackett appears on the Johnny Carson Show and does his stand-
up routine, he looks directly at the camera, since he is playing to
the audience out there in TV land. But notice that when he sits
down on the couch he rarely, if ever, looks at the camera. He looks
at Johnny, he looks at Ed McMahon, he looks at the studio audience or other guests. But never at the camera.

5. Just before going on the set, slowly drink some warm coffee or tea. It's an old actor's trick for loosening the vocal chords. It might prevent your voice from sounding squeaky and nervous.

6. And for heaven's sake, speak slowly! A headlong rush of words tripping all over themselves is perhaps second only to a high-register squeak as a telltale sign of nervousness. Remember, the viewer out there does not understand that you're not a professional and therefore have a right to be a little nervous. At best, your nervousness will just get in the way of effectively getting your message across. At worst, it may give the viewer the idea that you are insincere or maybe even that you are not telling the truth!

7. Sit up straight! Don't slouch. This, to be sure, sounds like advice from your mother, but it's valid all the same. For some reason I'll never fathom, people tend to slouch when they are on one of those living room sets. And it usually makes them look like frogs. Scoot your posterior as far back in the chair as you can, straighten your back, and hold your head up. You'll look ten years younger.

8. For men, watch those collars and jacket buttons. Another reason not to slouch is that if you do, a large shoulder-to-shoulder roll will automatically appear just behind the collar of your coat. Not only does it ruin the line of a good suit or sportscoat, it makes your neck disappear, which has the effect of adding twenty pounds to your weight. Maybe the proverbial ninety-eight-pound weakling would like to add twenty pounds, but most of the rest of us wouldn't. Keeping your jacket buttoned when you're seated also has the same effect.

So, men, just before you sit down, unbottom your coat and smooth down the back of your jacket by running your hands downward over your seat, starting at the small of the back.

9. For women, if you're wearing a business suit, follow the advice just given for men. If you're wearing a dress, make sure the hemline is sufficiently long that it covers your knees when you're seated. Just as you don't want any "hip shots" when you're speaking, you don't want any "hip shots" when the camera is pointed in your direction either.

10. Finally, use visuals! I've said this before, of course, but it's worth emphasizing. TV is a visual medium. If you don't prepare

something visual, other than a talking head or two, then you have ignored one of TV's greatest strengths. Photo prints (8 × 10's at least) are better than nothing. A flip chart is fine. Slides are good. A well done videotape is better. A live demonstration is better yet.

DEALING WITH CONTROVERSY

My friend Ned was a guest on a local radio phone-in show. He is a long-term member of a local bicycle club that has several hundred members. His appearance was scheduled to help promote an upcoming major cross-country ride the group sponsored early each summer. He also talked about bicycle safety, about how bicycling can help keep you fit, about the rising popularity of biking, and he even told humorous anecdotes about previous rides.

The phone-in callers cooperated by asking questions that solicited positive answers about the fun and healthiness of bicycling. Then one caller threw Ned a real curveball. "Why," the caller asked, "would any *decent* person want to join that bicycle club, since it's only an excuse for those people to sleep around with each other?"

Ned was so totally taken by surprise by this extremely loaded question that there was a second or two of "dead air" (silence), in which, I suspect, he and the talk show host stared at each other in utter disbelief. Ned mumbled a weak denial of the allegation and the host cut to a commercial.

What might Ned have done? He should have seized the initiative and turned this extremely negative question into a positive.

For example, he might have cited the fact that there were several ministers and their wives among the membership of the club, as well as numerous prominent community leaders, and that these outstanding citizens were unlikely to belong to a group involved in anything unethical.

He might also have gone on to point out that doctors often "prescribe" joining a bicycle club to their patients as an enjoyable way of losing weight and improving their cardiovascular health.

Another friend once claimed that all managers practice "creative paranoia," which he defined as "always hoping for the best, but expecting the worst." Approaching an appearance on a TV or radio talk show, where there is always the chance of getting some totally off-the-wall question thrown at you, with "creative paranoia" may be the smartest thing you can do.

If you do get one of those curveball questions, here's how to handle it:

1. Return to your talking points. Stress the positive, as my friend might have by stressing the upstanding people who are members of his bicycle club.

2. Use the old politician's ploy of answering the question you *wish* had been asked rather than the one that was. Why, for instance, would people want to join the bicycle club? To keep fit and to improve their health, of course.

3. Even though your gut reaction is to indignantly deny the aspersion, don't! Unfortunately, after Watergate and similar scandals, people have become rather cynical about categorical denials. For every two or three who accept the denial as true, there will be one who says, "Aha! That caller sure touched a nerve. Must be some truth in it!" Deflect the attack by keeping cool and staying in control.

4. If you are completely thrown off guard, then say so. Buy a little time to ponder your answer. You can grab a few extra seconds with the old standard "That's a very good question," or, "I'm glad someone asked that question."

5. If, by some chance, the question seems to have substance and actually deserves a thoughtful answer, then say something like "That's a very sensitive question you've asked and I certainly want to respond to it. But I don't feel it's appropriate to do so on the air. If you'll please hold the line, during the next commercial break I'd be happy to talk with you further."

6. Never put down or otherwise insult the questioner, which may be your second gut instinct. Don Rickles can get away with this in his nightclub act, but you are not Don Rickles, and the studio is not a nightclub. In this situation, just follow the old rule of "if you can't say something nice (about the questioner), don't say anything at all."

Getting Started Tomorrow Morning

Do you watch "Meet the Press," "This Week with David Brinkley," or the "McLaughlin Group" on Sunday mornings? Watch them with "new eyes" now.

Watch how well the guests seem to answer extremely complex questions in twenty-five words or less. Literally count the words to see what I mean.

Watch how they deflect a tough question by only partially answering it, by changing the subject, or by answering the question they wished had been asked rather than the one that was.

Watch how they somehow always return to the same three or four major themes—their talking points—no matter what questions have been asked.

As I've suggested before, to master a skill you have to practice it. "Produce" your own talk show about your small business, agency, or group. Do it on you own by renting a video camera and VCR from a local rental shop. Have journalism students from a local high school be the media representatives. And be sure to encourage them to ask some tough questions.

Or contact the mass communications or journalism department of a nearby community college, trade school, or four-year college, and find out if they have a TV or radio studio. Ask if they would be willing to "produce" a talk/interview show as a lab experience for their students.

9

Don't Ignore the
Nonmajor Media

U p to this point I have concentrated almost entirely on how you can maximize the impact of your publicity efforts through the so-called major media in your community. These are the local network-affiliated on-the-air TV channels, the AM and FM radio stations, and the daily or weekly newspaper(s) that cover your area. They are clearly the principal sources of local information for most of your community and, as such, deserve the lion's share of your efforts.

However, this does not mean that you should ignore the so-called nonmajor or nontraditional media. "Nonmajor" is a kind of umbrella term that encompasses all sorts of strange media. These can run the gamut from a local retiree club's newsletter to the local educational TV station, from a free-distribution neighborhood weekly newspaper to a closed circuit TV channel "broadcast" only within a hospital, from a Spanish-language FM radio station to a local-origination cable TV channel run by a church, from an internal company house organ to a trade magazine published strictly for people in your industry.

FRAGMENTATION COMES TO THE MEDIA

Once upon a time, if you got an article in the local paper and a mention on one or two of the local network-affiliated TV channels' late evening newscasts, you could be all but certain that virtually everyone you wanted to see your message did, indeed, see it. On any given day, 90 percent or more of the households in most communities read the paper or watched an evening newscast. For many years the major local media were that dominant!

Much to the chagrin of the owners and management of these media, however, to say nothing of their ad or circulation sales departments, this is not as true as it used to be. Fragmentation is hitting the media like a runaway freight train.

Media fragmentation means that:

• Instead of faithfully watching the 10 or 11 o'clock newscast every night, today's TV viewer may now be tuned to a sports event or a concert on one of the cable channels or may have rented a movie for the VCR. Or he or she may not even have the TV on because of working late or attending a community meeting of some sort.

• Instead of thoroughly reading the local paper every day, front to back, as they once did, today's readers may scan the main news sections, stopping to read only selected articles, and may out and out skip whole sections. And they may even skip a day or two a week because they're "too busy."

• Instead of listening exclusively to their favorite radio station on the way to and from work, or perhaps even all day, today's radio listeners may punch preprogrammed selection buttons to skip from station to station, avoiding commercials and/or newscasts, or may even be listening to a motivational tape on their tape deck instead of to the radio.

Just to keep things in perspective, the fact is, the local major media—the daily or weekly hometown newspaper, the network-affiliated TV channels, the AM and FM radio stations—are still by far the dominant source most people turn to for local information, and will probably continue to be so for years to come. However, it is also likely that in most markets there will be a growing number of small, specialty media that you ought to be aware of, especially if your product or service is targeted at a specific consumer segment.

Over the last few years, there has been a steady increase in the number and quality of these specialty media that serve small, highly targeted segments of the community, even at the local level. There are five very important reasons why you should include these smaller, nonmajor media in your publicity programs:

1. Your business, agency, or group may at some time have a particularly strong interest in reaching a certain narrowly focused community segment, and one of these specialty media might be the most efficient way for you to accomplish your goal.

For example, if you're a health care agency about to offer some new program of specific interest to people over the age of sixty, while you will certainly send news releases to the major media, you may well want to develop a more in-depth article for the weekly paper or monthly magazine that is targeted at seniors.

2. As a general rule, it is easier to get more extensive coverage in one of these media, especially as compared to the major media, so long as your information is specifically of interest to the group being targeted.

Using the senior health program example again, the major media will probably give you a brief mention of your new program without much problem, but may balk at heavier coverage because they think the mature market is too small a portion of their total audience. The tabloid newspaper that serves this market exclusively, however, will probably give you all the coverage you want.

3. In some very large urban markets, the so-called local major media are so large that they are, in effect, as inaccessible to a small business, agency, or volunteer group as a network news shot or *Time* cover.

It isn't likely that WNBC, the New York City local NBC affiliate, is going to cover the grand opening of a new deli restaurant over in Brooklyn. However, there may be a weekly (or even daily) newspaper, perhaps a low-power independent TV station, and one or more radio stations that all specialize in coverage of Brooklyn news that *would* show up for the new deli's grand opening.

4. Because markets are becoming so fragmented, you may have to turn to these specialty media to reach everyone you want to reach.

Let's take our illustration of the program for seniors a step further. Let's assume that it is especially targeted at the poor elderly. It's entirely possible that the poorest of these people do not subscribe to the local paper and maybe don't even own a TV. So all the excellent coverage the traditional media may give your new program could be worthless if you are not in fact reaching one of your important target segments. However, these same poor people regularly read the free-distribution shoppers and senior publications they can pick up in most drug stores, food stores, or senior centers.

It's no different with businesses. Let's say you're a retail shoe shop that specializes in heavy-duty work shoes and boots. You've just landed the exclusive area franchise for a new line of work boots that are industry-specific; for instance, one of your boots is designed for utility linemen and others who work around high voltage because it can protect the wearer against up to 20,000 volts. A news release should be sent to the local newspaper and will probably get a one- or two-paragraph mention on the business page. And maybe some of your potential customers will see that one brief mention in the paper.

But to make sure of reaching your potential customers, you would be wise to send a copy of the news release to the house organs of the local electric utility company, the telephone company, and any other large manufacturers who employ electricians, as well as to the newsletter of the local chapter of the IBEW (International Brotherhood of Electrical Workers).

5. There is a tendency for people to feel that local media are more credible. Over the years there's been lots of talk about which media and/or which network anchorperson people trust the most. It's an axiom in journalism: The closer an individual medium is to the audience it serves—either geographically, like a weekly newspaper serving a specific suburb, or by life-style or interest, for example a monthly magazine for model railroad buffs—the more believable it is to that audience.

Mostly Print

With the near-universal availability of neighborhood quick print shops, high-quality copying machines, inexpensive bulk postage rates, and the booming interest in and affordability of personal computer-based desktop publishing systems, most of the specialty media in the coming years will probably be in some form of print.

That's not a surprise. Despite all the talk about print becoming obsolete in the Information Age, most people still prefer to hold something solid in their hands when reading; they like to be able to set it aside and think about what they've read and to pick it up again later to reread.

Also, if serving small, specifically targeted audiences is the goal, then print, of all the media, lends itself most easily to carefully controlling distribution through the mail or by hand delivery.

However, don't be surprised to see all sorts of unique new media emerging over the next few years, from electronic "bulletin boards" accessed by personal computers to low-power TV stations serving specific neighborhoods.

TARGETING

There are three basic ways in which specialty media try to target themselves:

1. *By geography.* In effect, these media claim to serve the information needs of an audience living within specific geographic boundaries—perhaps a neighborhood, a city, a suburb, or even a county. This category includes such familiar media as hometown radio stations and small-town weeklies.

2. *By life-style/life cycle.* This group of media tries to identify the behavioral and demographic characteristics of certain groups, such as "young singles" or "senior citizens," and to serve the specialized information needs of that particular group.

Well-known national media that fit this category are magazines like *Family Circle,* targeted at women with small children, and *Modern Maturity,* which is targeted at people over fifty-five.

At the local level, this category might include a magazine that stresses what's happening in the community on the entertainment scene—plays, concerts, restaurants, nightclubs. . . .

You should also recognize that this category includes a number of cable TV channels, for example, the Lifetime channel, which stresses health topics, and CBN, which carries a lot of family and religious programming.

3. *By special interest.* This category includes trade publications, such as magazines directed specifically at golf equipment retailers or metallurgical engineers; hobbyist publications, for stamp collectors, craftspeople, model railroaders, and the like;

and a kind of miscellaneous category that includes everything from "fan mags," providing gossip on soap opera or rock stars, to hunting and fishing publications.

Sometimes a specific medium has one foot in two different categories. For example, is a body-building magazine a life-style publication or a special interest magazine? It's probably both.

The point isn't that you can neatly pigeonhole each individual medium, but rather that you should understand that there is a fundamental difference between a medium that defines its role as providing *all* of the informational needs of a large and diverse audience in a given geographic area—such as a local TV station or newspaper does—and a medium that defines its role as serving the information needs of a very specific and narrowly focused group.

TWO DOZEN "OTHER GUYS" WORTH LOOKING INTO

Here's a checklist of two dozen nonmajor media you should look into. Obviously not all these will be present in every community; nor will all of them necessarily be appropriate for you to use. Rather, the purpose of this checklist is to help you to look past the obvious choices—the daily newspaper or TV station—and dig into your market to find those specialized media that might offer you some unique opportunities for exposure.

1. *News/talk radio.* If there are more than two AM radio stations in your market, chances are that one of them is a news/talk format station. While this is certainly part of one of the major media, radio, I've included the talk portion here because guest appearances on radio talk shows are handled differently from routine releases.

The big-name talk shows—Donohue, Larry King, Bruce Williams—are generated nationally. But most news/talk stations have at least one locally originated phone-in show. And, generally speaking, they are always looking for guests. Doing a guest shot on a local talk show isn't for everyone, but it is certainly an underutilized opportunity for exposure for many local businesses and volunteer groups (see Chapter 8 for ideas on how to wangle a guest appearance on a local radio or TV talk show and how to handle yourself when you do.)

2. *Neighborhood or community tabloids.* Most urban areas of any size have a daily newspaper that serves the entire community. Underneath this umbrella daily, however, are often one or more small newspaperlike publications that serve a certain neighborhood or suburban area.

Their niche is to supply news and information that is very specific to their neighborhood or community. Finding an angle that makes your news release relevant to that neighborhood or community is the key to getting coverage here. They are usually supported by local ads and are distributed free at pickup points throughout the area they serve. Look for them in supermarkets and drugstores and even on street corners.

3. *Local-origination channels on cable TV.* Check to see if your local cable TV distributor has what's called a local access channel. When cable first began to sweep across the country a little over a decade ago, local access was supposed to suddenly make the vast power of television available to a great diversity of local interest groups at little or no cost. Of course, it hasn't quite worked out on the grand scale originally envisioned. But, as the years pass, more and more of these channels come on line, either sponsored by the cable company itself or by a local college or some other nonprofit group. They will generally have talk/interview shows. And, if they're connected with a college that has a TV studio, they may even be producing some local documentaries. They are definitely worth checking out.

4. *Local educational TV channels.* These over-the-air channels are also generally sponsored by a local college or school district, but are sometimes sponsored by an independent, not-for-profit corporation. While most local educational TV channels do not do regular local news broadcasts, they often do have local talk/ interview shows and/or produce local documentaries. If you have one in your community, it's worth getting to know.

5. *Local public radio stations.* Similarly, these stations are usually operated by a local college. They often feature jazz, folk, or classical music, but do carry a large amount of public service pro-

gramming, including locally originated news, interviews, and discussion programs.

6. *Local business publications.* At first only a phenomenon of the very largest urban areas, local business publications in one form or another can now be seen in communities as small as 25,000 or 30,000. The more sophisticated versions are published weekly or biweekly and use four-color photos and premium-quality print. Smaller areas may have monthly or quarterly publications printed on newsprint. In any case, such a local publication should definitely be on your media list. It will always publish your routine news announcements and will often be very interested in feature articles about your business, its products, and services.

7. *Local city magazines.* Many communities or regions have what in the trade is called a "city magazine," which tends to be heavy on local life-style feature stories and local retail advertising. In most cases, these publications are targeted at an upscale audience. They almost always include calendars of community events and often carry feature articles on prominent people and/or community organizations.

8. *Local entertainment guides.* These weekly or monthly publications are generally targeted at a young crowd and stress reviews of restaurants, plays, concerts, and nightclubs. But they also carry calendars of community events and sometimes feature special events.

9. *Local tourism guides.* These publications, which can vary from very slick, four-color magazines to newspaper-style tabloids, are big on community calendars and special events. They are a must if your event or activity is a major community affair.

10. *Ethnic publications.* These are often similar in look to the neighborhood/community newspapers mentioned above, but tend to focus on the life-style or culture of a specific ethnic group. They are often published in a foreign language. Include them on your media list if your business or agency serves this group or if your activities are of special interest to it.

11. *Senior citizen newsletters and newspapers.* There are two kinds to look for here. In some communities there is a tabloidlike newspaper, usually a monthly, distributed free at supermarkets and elsewhere. It tends to carry features on health, personal fi-

nance, Social Security, and retirement, but also often has articles on travel and local events.

The other kind is the newsletter published by the local chapter of a specific senior group, such as the American Association of Retired Persons (AARP) or a union retiree's group. This kind tends to stress issues and legislation.

In either case, the so-called mature market is taking on increasing importance in terms both of its economic power and its political clout. Is it important to you?

12. *Local high school or college newspapers.* At the other end of the spectrum, if reaching a youth audience is important to your group or business, maybe you should look into developing a feature article for these publications.

13. *Chamber of Commerce newsletters.* Just about every community has its own chamber of commerce and each one has some form of newsletter for its membership. While many are little more than copy machine duplicates of a typewriter-style sheet, some are quite professionally done. In any event, they all contain articles about the activities and accomplishments of their members. If you're a member, you should be represented on a regular basis.

14. *Various local specialty publications.* These can include tabloid newspapers for labor or union groups, a diocesan newspaper, a newsletter directed at members of a particular political party, computer users' group newsletters. . . . The list is virtually endless.

15. *Local club bulletins or newsletters.* Whether they cater to stamp collectors or horseback riders, runners or model airplane builders, mountain climbers or dahlia growers, just about every local club of any size publishes its own membership newsletter. Why are these groups important? If you're a garden center, maybe the dahlia society would be interested in running an article by you about the newest insecticides on the market. If you're a shoe store, maybe the local hiking club would be interested in a brief article on the latest in high-tech, lightweight hiking shoes.

16. *Local service club bulletins.* Local service groups are normally heavily dominated by men and women in the business and professional area, which is always a worthwhile audience to tar-

get. Even though they tend to focus exclusively on their own members and organizational activities in their bulletins, there might be an occasion when you could develop a profile on one of your employees who is also a member of the group.

17. *Newspapers or newsletters published on local federal installations or military bases.* The larger the facility, the more professional in quality will be its publication. Why might you want to reach this audience? If you're in the financial industry, maybe you could develop a feature story about how annuities and the federal retirement program can complement one another.

18. *Local low-power TV channels or low-power radio stations.* This is something new. Like the neighborhood or community newspaper, these are designed to meet the specialized informational needs of a limited area. At present, they will be found only in the very largest urban areas, but, like cable's local access channel, as the concept becomes more popular they will pop up in smaller and smaller markets.

19. *Closed circuit TV channels.* You will most likely find these serving a hospital or a college campus. How might you use them? If you sell or rent home health care supplies, I'll bet that several of the manufacturers you buy from have developed how-to videos about their equipment. I'll also bet that for a relatively small fee they would insert the name and phone number of your business at the end of their tape. Finally, I'd bet that the local hospital with a closed circuit channel might be very interested in showing your tapes. You couldn't ask for a more captive audience!

20. *Newspapers, magazines, or newsletters published by local companies for their customers.* Of course these publications are created by companies to promote their own products or services. And of course they aren't likely to allow a competitor to have an article in their publication. But if your product or service somehow complements or enhances theirs, that could be a different story. For example, a local retailer of lawn mowers and other power garden equipment might let you, a retailer of garden supplies, write an article for his newsletter on how and when to use lawn fertilizers.

21. *Newsletters published by the local schools or the city.* No, they probably wouldn't be too happy if you blatantly tried to sell

your product. But if your firm or some of its employees helped build a playground for neighborhood kids, you might just get a photo with a mention of your business, agency, or group in the caption.

22. *Local computer "bulletin boards."* This is a new and unique medium that is certainly worth investigating if you have anything to do with computers.

23. *Internal company employee publications.* These more or less traditional house organs vary from plain, mimeograph-style to very sophisticated magazine-approach publications. Say you're a new fitness center specializing in low-impact aerobics. You write a 200- to 250-word article on the benefits of low-impact aerobics, putting a byline on it that reads "By Sally Jones, Suburban Fitness Center." You send out a couple dozen copies addressed to "Employee Newsletter Editor" at the largest employers in your area. Only six of them actually use the article in their company newsletter, but those six reach over 10,000 employees. How much was that exposure worth in terms of the equivalent out-of-pocket cost for advertising by direct mail to reach those 10,000 people?

24. *Area singles publications.* Many communities have publications directed at singles. Some have a specific age orientation; others may target people of a certain religion. Human service and counseling agencies, especially, should be aware of these publications and their editorial criteria. But so should insurance agencies, fitness centers, and other enterprises.

WHAT ABOUT TRADE PUBLICATIONS?

As mentioned in the introduction, the principal focus of this book is on helping you to develop your publicity programs in local media. However, there is one category of specialized media that, while not usually local, does belong on your media list. These are the trade publications and professional journals directed at specific industries and even segments within those industries.

The variety of these publications is almost unbelievable, in terms of both their style and quality. Every industry has at least one, and usually several.

At a minimum, you should routinely send the same news release that goes to the local media to the trade publications in your industry. On occasion, you may even want to customize a news release specifically for the trade publications, lengthening it, perhaps going into more technical detail than you would for the general media.

Why should you worry about getting coverage in trade publications of your industry? The best reason of all for businesses to appear as often as they can in trade publications is that customers and *potential* customers see it. If it's true, as I suggested earlier, that getting exposure in the local media helps legitimize your business, agency, or group, then this is doubly true of an appearance in a trade publication.

If a favorable article does appear in a trade publication about your business or one of its products or services, I would certainly quickly make reprints—first securing permission from the magazine, of course—and then send them out to customers and include them in all future media kits.

Getting Started Tomorrow Morning

Not all media are necessarily right for your specific business, agency, or group. So, the first step in effectively using them is to define your target groups. (For more detailed information on identifying and prioritizing target groups, see Chapter 12).

Once you have some sense of your target market segments, then you can begin to construct a list of the specialty media that might reach them. For some segments the specialty media will be fairly obvious.

But in some cases you may need to dig a little deeper, perhaps conduct a telephone survey. One basic approach is to call at least a hundred people in the target group and ask them what media they pay attention to. You'll probably have to prompt them by providing a list of specifically named media with a yes/no option. Of course, you also need to give them an open-ended question so that they can name media that aren't on the list.

You might also survey major employers and/or businesses in your area to find out if they have employee or customer publications and to learn who is in charge of them. Ask for a sample issue if you really think there might be some possibilities there.

Don't ask them if they accept contributions from outside sources, because you will probably get an automatic "no." Rather, wait until you have a specific and well-thought-out idea before contacting the editor to see if he or she is interested.

10

What to Do When the
Media Are After Your Hide

The major thrust of this book is that you should adopt a *positive,* proactive publicity stance. Virtually every group, agency, or business has many untold stories that would be of interest to readers and viewers. I've suggested that, in today's highly competitive, information-loaded marketplace, you *must* constantly be building a "bank account" of positive images with your customers, clients, contributors, members, and anyone else who's important to you. And I've tried to give you lots of specific suggestions on how to implement this strategy.

There can also be a downside to publicity. Every once in a while something happens that suddenly propels you or your business or organization into the white-hot glare of media attention, usually when it's the *last* thing you want!

WHEN NIGHTMARES COME TRUE

Just let your imagination run wild for a moment. From a public relations viewpoint, what's the *worst* thing that could happen to your organization?

Let's pretend:

• You're the owner and CEO of a small electronic component assembly plant. You've received an official notification from your state environmental protection agency that the old dump at the back of your plant site, which was left over from the now-bankrupt firm from which you bought the building, is full of toxic wastes.

It'll cost at least $2 million to clean it up and the state agency wants you to file your cleanup plan in thirty days or face fines! The announcement by the state agency has moved over the state wire service, and several local TV stations are calling to ask if they can send a camera crew to take pictures of "your toxic dump" and interview you about "your pollution problem."

• You're the exec of a long-established community agency that serves youth. The local joint community charitable campaign has fallen 25 percent short of its fund-raising goal. A hastily called campaign board meeting was held last night and it was decided that some, supposedly more direct service agencies would not be cut at all, while others—including yours—would face a 50 percent reduction in their funding from the joint community campaign. A reporter for the daily paper is on the phone asking how many staff members you're going to lay off and how many potentially troubled youth clients you will turn away in view of this severe cutback.

• You're the president of a local luncheon service club. Once a year your club sponsors a casino night and auction as its major fund-raising activity for community projects. The event usually raises between $15,000 and $20,000—$5,000-plus of it in cash. A week has passed since the event. Last night the planning committee held a wrap-up meeting, at which there was to have been a general discussion of how the event went and a final report of income. But the treasurer didn't show up—and has not been seen or heard from since the event. No one seems to know where the treasurer or the cash went. You've just spent most of the day at the police station telling them what little you know about the treasurer's personal habits and personal problems. Now, just as you think they're finished and you'll get to go home, the detective sergeant says, "Oh, by the way, there's a half dozen reporters and TV cameras out there waiting to talk to you."

Sound farfetched? It can't happen to you? Don't believe it. Three Mile Island and Chernobyl couldn't happen either, but they did!

The fact is, every business, agency, and group, big or small, is subject to being hit by a crisis—unexpected emergency situations like fires or tornadoes, unanticipated controversies like running afoul of some government regulation or a labor dispute, and personal tragedies like the CEO being involved in an accident or running off with his secretary. When you're caught completely unprepared because the disaster is so unexpected, confusion runs rampant. Rumors and half-truths get reported as fact. Unnamed "sources" tell conflicting or contradictory stories to the media. Day after day the media reveal some embarrassing new finding, until you think there's nothing left of your image in the community or of your reputation among customers, clients, or contributors.

The Media at Their Worst

Most of the time your relationships with the media will be emotionally neutral. If you're lucky, and you've taken the time to build a rapport with reporters and editors, they can be friendly and sometimes even helpful. Until a disaster befalls you or your business. Then, like wolves that smell blood, they allow their most carnivorous instincts to take over.

Friendship and past relationships go out the window. "Getting the story" becomes the all-important mission. Getting it ahead of everyone else is better yet. And this is not just a trait of the national media. Even the usually friendly and accommodating local reporter can suddenly shift into a "Mike Wallace mode" when there is the smell of controversy or wrongdoing in the air.

Ask anyone who's been there. There is nothing more intimidating than facing a pack of reporters when you're not used to it, especially when, because of some controversy or accusation, you're on the defensive. No, they don't literally snarl, but you think at any time they're going to! The TV lights are bright and glaring, like the cliché in the spy movies, "You *will* answer our questions!" The technicians, with their cables and microphones, go about hooking you up as if they were strapping you into the electric chair. There are no friendly faces, no reassuring smiles.

So, how *do* you respond when the cameras are rolling and the videotape machine is recording and a reporter sticks a microphone in your face and demands an answer to the equivalent of the proverbial "Tell me, are you *still* beating your wife?"

TWELVE TIPS ON DEALING WITH HOSTILE MEDIA

For the purpose of illustration, let's assume your relationships with the media under a crisis situation will be hostile. Which is to say adversarial at best, and downright belligerent at worst. Here are twelve techniques you can use to blunt that hostility and even to turn it around and use it to your advantage:

1. *Above all, you must seize control of the situation.* Both the immediate situation, which is the confrontation with one or more reporters, and the overall situation that is the cause of the crisis. I'll have more to say on this latter aspect in a minute.

Why is getting control of the relationship with the press so important? First, the last thing you want is for your personal image or the image of your business, agency, or group to come across in the media as tentative and defensive. Depending on the situation, such an image could have all sorts of unfavorable repercussions with your customers, clients, or contributors, to say nothing of regulators and/or legislators.

Second, you need to seize control because it is the only truly effective way you have to keep adverse information from getting out and/or to correct any misinformation that has gotten out.

2. *Identify one spokesperson to handle the crisis with the media.* It's part of keeping control. If you have one designated source of information for the media, you can coordinate information through that spokesperson and you won't have other sources of potentially conflicting or contradictory statements talking to the media.

The higher up in the organization the spokesperson is, the better. While it's great if that person is articulate and comfortable in front of cameras, always remember that in the eyes of the media and the public alike the CEO has much more credibility than "a PR hack." Establishing credibility is very important.

3. *Make sure that your spokesperson [possibly yourself] is accessible to the media.* Take their phone calls, even though it's the ninth one of the morning and you know you're going to be asked the same questions for the umpteenth time. If the situation is se-

rious enough, hold daily news conferences to provide progress reports. In a crisis situation, it simply can't be business as usual, so stop trying to act as if it is.

Once again, you do not want to give even the slightest hint that you are trying to conceal something from the media or the public. If you do, that's like waving the proverbial red cape in front of a bull. If the media have the slightest inkling that you're hiding something, they will dig and dig, they will call every source they can think of, they will piece together half-truths and rumors and go with what they perceive is the story you are trying to cover up.

4. *Besides being accessible, be honest!* If you don't know the answer to a reporter's question, say so. Promise to get the answer and, of course, deliver on that promise. Never bluff. It'll be found out. And when it is, you've lost both credibility and control.

5. *Never, never say "no comment!"* Both to the media and the public at large, that's a tacit admission of guilt. A "no comment" automatically translates as "I'm hiding something embarrassing."

If you can't comment because regulations don't permit it, for example, SEC rules, then say so. If you can't comment because you've not yet seen some specific report or document, then say so. But then go on to say when you expect to receive the report and when you expect to have a statement on it ready.

6. *Always remember that in a crisis or controversy there is no such thing as "off the record."* Always assume that if you say it, it will end up on page one the next day.

7. *Don't become the victim of intimidation.* At the national level, like an NFL linebacker, the media tend to use intimidation as a matter of routine. While local media are a bit less practiced at this game than their network cousins, they are still much better at it than you are. Insofar as possible, you should not let them play their intimidation games on you.

One of the best ways to prevent this is by always responding to their negative and hostile questions with positive answers. By ignoring their attack, by not letting them put you on the defensive, you blunt or deflect the attack.

You can also take a lesson from the politicians and answer the question you *wish* the reporter had asked instead of the one he actually did ask. People always remember the answer you give, rarely the question that was asked.

8. *If you're going into a formal news conference, always have a brief statement prepared in advance.* You should always read this statement for the record, even though both you and the media know that they will use only a ten- or fifteen-second clip from it at most.

The reason you should read the statement is that it is a key part of your effort to get control. By reading a statement you are able, at least in part, to set some of the ground rules and to establish the tone of the follow-up questions. Of course you should always have plenty of copies of your statement to hand out to each reporter.

9. *In addition to having a formal statement, you should also develop several major talking points.* Talking points are what you stress when you answer questions. These should be no more than one- or two-sentence summaries. The best way to identify potential talking points is to ask yourself, "What are the *good* points the media are ignoring or not stressing?" Talking points are for your use; you don't distribute copies to the media.

10. *Rehearse.* Read over your statement out loud in front of a mirror at least a dozen or so times until you have virtually memorized it. Again, to the degree possible, you want to look as if you are comfortable and in control in front of the cameras. What you should do is look directly at the camera or the reporters and talk in a conversational tone, only glancing briefly at your text. What you *don't* want is to be seen on camera with downcast eyes, nervously reading a prepared statement.

If you have time, ask friends or associates to throw questions at you. Tell them they should be the nastiest questions they can think of, the "Are you still beating your wife?" variety. They are definitely *not* doing you any favors by sparing your feelings and tossing you nothing but cream puffs.

11. *In addition to the formal statement you hand out, you should also give reporters a full copy of your regular media kit about your business or agency.* If you don't have a regular media kit, then besides your formal statement you should prepare a

separate backgrounder news release or fact sheet about your business, agency, or organization, telling what you do, when you were established, how many people you employ, and so forth. Once again, it's all part of presenting yourself in the most positive manner possible and of giving every appearance that you are being open and forthcoming with information.

12. *Finally, prepare in advance.* If you wait until a crisis situation hits to plan for how you're going to respond, it's too late. While big companies have crisis management plans that can run to hundreds of pages, even the smallest business, agency, or organization should have some sort of plan, even if it's only a one-page memo that's distributed to all key employees and updated once a year.

ADVOCACY AND SPECIAL INTEREST GROUPS

Another kind of worst-case scenario to look out for is one that involves some special interest or advocacy group generating media attention on your organization by picketing, issuing a critical report, or showing up before a governmental body to oppose some proposal you've made or to accuse you of not living up to some rule or regulation.

Like it or not, these groups are a fact of life in today's consumer-sensitized marketplace and there is no sign they are about to go away. In fact, if anything, there is every indication that there will be more, not less, of such groups clustering around all sorts of odd issues in the years ahead.

Remember, the media thrive on conflict and revel in dramatizing a Good Guys versus Bad Guys scenario. The media, of course, like to believe that they are only reporting objectively on conflict that is already there; others believe that their strident style of coverage may help to create that conflict in the first place. Regardless, from a public relations standpoint, you do *not* want to get sucked into that conflict because you *can't* win. Even if the facts will eventually vindicate your position, take my advice and steer clear of conflict.

The vindication will not receive anywhere near the media attention the original confrontation did, and, therefore, lots of people will never know you were in the right all along. Even if they see the story of your vindication, there will always be those who believe you weaseled out of it somehow.

Suppose you do adopt a hard-nosed attitude toward the media and those "nuts" who are attacking you. You issue terse, technically oriented news releases that really don't say much. You refuse one-on-one interview requests. You restrict where reporters and camera crews can go. You don't supply any unnecessary background information on who you are and what you do. You only issue statements through a public relations spokesperson.

Suppose this time you are successful in weathering the storm by not giving in to the "kooks" and by not revealing anything to the media. The fact is, you didn't win, you lost. You lost credibility with the media. You lost the goodwill of the community.

And both groups have very long memories. So the next time you're invovled in some sort of controversy—and never doubt, there *will* be a next time—the media will come after you with even sharper teeth. And people in the community will say to themselves, "Just as I thought, where there's smoke there's fire."

That's why your media strategy, especially in a controversy generated by a special interest or advocacy group, must in every possible way give both the *appearance* and the *substance* of being open, cooperative, and communicative. You must never look as if you are dragging your heels, or, to use a term popularized by Watergate, "stonewalling." That's what Richard Nixon tried, and it eventually cost him his job.

DEVELOPING A BASIC CRISIS MEDIA PLAN

Here's how to develop a basic crisis media plan *before* you need one.

Once a year get all your key people together for a couple of hours to brainstorm some worst-case scenarios. What do you hope will never happen to your group, agency, or business? A fire or tornado destroys your business? You're slapped with a lawsuit or citation for breaking some regulation? The CEO keels over from a heart attack? There's an injury or industrial accident? Someone embezzles money?

Of course a list of these terrible "what if's" could be very lengthy. But through brainstorming and discussion, what you should be trying to do is to identify the half dozen or so potential crises to which you are the most vulnerable and which would have the most devastating impact on your business or group. Remember, vulnerability to and impact of are the two key elements.

As specifically as you can, talk about the possible internal and external effects of these crises. How would it affect your employees, your operations, your delivery schedules, your income? What impact would it have on your customers, clients, members, or contributors? What would the community's response be? And how would the media react?

Then discuss as specifically as you can what *your* response should be. The results of this discussion become your crisis management plan. For the purposes of this book, I will focus only on the portion of your plan dealing with the media, although you should remember that there are many more elements than just public relations involved in effective crisis management planning.

The media portion of your crisis plan should include:

- The names of the persons within your organization who are to be notified in the event of a crisis, together with their work and home phone numbers. In corporate crisis plans this group is usually called the crisis management team.
- The name or title of the person who is authorized to call news conferences and release information to the media; a designated backup person in case the authorized person is out of town or otherwise unavailable; and the work and home phone numbers of both.
- The name of the designated media spokesperson for your organization and that person's backup, plus their work and home phone numbers.
- The name of the person who is responsible for preparing news releases and coordinating information for the media, and the work and home numbers of this person if different from the spokesperson.
- A list of the names and phone numbers of all local news

media, plus any trade or out-of-town media important to you.

- The location of your organization's media kits.
- The place where a media conference of a dozen or more people could be held at your location or, if there is not enough room, where else it might be held.
- Any special instructions that might be specific to your operation, such as official agencies to be notified in case of a toxic spill.

The motto of the Boy Scouts of America is perhaps the single best piece of advice any business, agency, or group can follow in dealing with the media during a crisis: Be prepared!

Meeting a Crisis Head-on: A Case Study

Even if you're caught off guard, quick thinking and an energetic response may allow you to retrieve the situation. Here's how one company dealt with its media crisis. The events presented here really happened. Only the names of those involved have been changed.

The Big River Towboat Company is headquartered in a medium-size Midwestern city along the Mississippi River. It hauls grain, coal, scrap metal, fertilizer, and other bulk commodities in barges up and down the Mississippi and its tributaries.

Big River's river terminal is adjacent to a mainline railroad track and is only about four blocks away from the community's downtown area. The ground on which the terminal sits is leased from the city, as are virtually all the terminal facilities in the port area.

Big River wanted to expand its ability to do intermodal transfer of materials, that is, to transfer cargoes from rail to barge and from barge to rail. To do this it needed to build a railroad spur from the main track down to the edge of the river and to add a large-capacity crane.

Because Big River's lease was up in five years, the company felt it needed a longer time to amortize the cost of the new construction, and so formally asked the city for a fifteen-year extension of its lease.

The expansion would enhance the community's competitive position as a river port and would also create jobs. It was Big River's expectation that its lease extension request would be handled routinely.

At a public hearing on the request for the lease extension, however, the Citizens' River Development Advisory Committee, a group created by the city that included a number of prominent community leaders, appeared in opposition to the extension.

The committee argued that industrial use was not the "highest and best use" of the valuable riverfront land and that it should eventually be developed as a mixed-use project with hotels, unique shopping areas, restaurants, and green space that would provide more access to the river for all citizens. In fact, the advisory committee not only suggested that Big River's lease extension request should be turned down but that the company should be ordered to vacate its leased land at the end of the current lease!

Big River was completely blindsided by this totally unexpected opposition. Company executives had thought of themselves as the good guys for wanting to bring economic growth and jobs to the community, not as the bad guys because they weren't using the land for its "highest and best use." Needless to say, the local media had a field day with this major controversy.

In brief, here's how Big River responded:

First and foremost, the company seized control of the situation. Two days after the public hearing, Big River held a news conference on the riverfront. It erected a tent to house the media. It made sure that there were several barges being loaded and unloaded nearby and had one of its towboats moving some barges around. In other words, the company presented the TV cameras with super visual images showing what a real working river looks like.

Second, rather than simply trying to refute the advisory group's position, in other words, responding from a defensive position, Big River went on the offensive. It developed a series of news releases describing in some detail the positive economic impact of its proposed terminal expansion, including reduced costs to local shippers, better access to international ports, the direct creation of new jobs at the expanded terminal, and the indirect creation of jobs through increased economic activity.

Big River was careful not to impugn the motives or honesty of the citizens' advisory committee as a group or of any of its individual members. Yet it was successfully able to turn the tables on the advisory committee because the media ended up characterizing the committee's position as being antijob and antieconomic development.

Third, Big River called on the most powerful spokesperson it could, the chairman of the board. It was certainly helpful that he was articulate and at ease in front of the cameras. Even more important, throughout the roughly week-long crisis period he put all his other activities on the back burner and made himself accessible to the media any time they called.

Finally, Big River developed an extensive media kit containing plenty of positive materials about the company, including:

- A full copy of the formal statement made by the chairman at the media conference.
- A summary news release on the entire situation.
- A backgrounder on the proposed terminal development, stressing the important long-term potential of the unique rail/barge intermodal facility, as well as detailing the specific short-term impact it would have in terms of new jobs.
- A backgrounder on the various studies and/or proposals for development of the riverfront that had been made by different groups over the years and how the new Big River proposal meshed with these previous studies.
- A fact sheet on the Big River Co.: when it was founded, how it had grown, how many it employed, how valuable it was to area shippers.
- A bio of the chairman.
- An historical backgrounder on the riverfront area and how it had been used continuously for industrial purposes from the days when sawmills were first built there in the 1850s.

Through aggressive use of the media and publicity, Big River by the end of the week was able to get the advisory committee to compromise on its no lease extension position—it agreed to a ten-year extension for Big River's lease—and to back away almost completely from its recommendation to terminate the lease entirely after five years; the committee now said that the Big River lease should be terminated only if and when a suitable alternative site was available. In short, Big River's preparations paid off and converted a near-catastrophe into a quasi-triumph.

Getting Started Tomorrow Morning

As you read the newspaper or watch television newscasts, start to take note of:

- How many stories are handled in a classic, objective manner, that is, with the elements of the story presented in an emotionally neutral, matter-of-fact fashion?
- How many stories are handled in a friendly manner, in which the basic approach to the news source is positive, perhaps even deferential?
- How many stories have an adversarial undertone, where the reporter's attitude seems to be that the source is trying to hide something and that it's his or her job to dig it out?

I bet you'll be surprised at the patterns that begin to emerge.

You'll find that very few stories fall into the objective, emotionally neutral category. This will be true whether the medium is local or national. Try as they may to achieve objectivity, most reporters write their stories with some kind of predetermined viewpoint. They can't help it.

You'll probably find that the majority of stories in the local media fall into the next category, that is, they tend to reflect a more positive attitude toward the news source. And conversely, you'll probably find that stories in the national media are much more likely to have an adversarial tone.

Because this is a chapter on how to handle yourself in a crisis situation, I'll suggest that you concentrate on those few local stories that are adversarial in nature and learn what you can from them.

For example, how did the local media handle the situation? Did they seem to take the spokesperson's statement at face value? Or did they press the attack, so to speak, and demand answers? Did they go to multiple sources for their information, or to only a limited few? For example, did they just quote someone who was pro and someone who was con? Or did they try to find a more or less objective source to put things in perspective?

How did the news sources handle themselves? Did they seem more or less at ease and in control? Did they give the impression that they were on top of the situation and that things were being taken care of? Or did you come away with the feeling that they weren't telling you everything and that there was more bad news to be revealed? Did they seem nervous and defensive? What, specifically, gave you this impression?

How long did the crisis tone in the media last? Was it over in one or two days, or did it drag on for a week? If it dragged on, why did it do so? What could the center of the controversy have done to get it over and done with in a day or two? Did the tone of the media change as the crisis continued? Did the tone become more or less strident?

Are some possible worst-case scenarios for your business, agency, or group starting to form in your mind? Are you now beginning to get a feel for what it would be like to face the media if one of those worst-case scenarios actually materialized? And are you working up a few ideas on how you might best handle yourself in one of those situations? Then you've taken the first few steps toward developing your crisis media plan!

11

Building Your Media File

If you're serious about wanting to get your share of publicity, then you'll have to start building a media contact file.

You've probably already got a Rolodex or its equivalent on your desk right next to the telephone. Mine not only includes the essentials, like names, addresses, and telephone numbers, but extra information, like the names of secretaries or receptionists who answer the phone, or the name of a contact's spouse, or key facts about someone's business or products. This extra information allows me to add a more personal touch to my conversation, when it seems appropriate; a receptionist whom I greet by name is far more likely to put me through.

A media file is the same thing except that it's focused on the media. If you can inquire after the health of a reporter's children by name, that reporter is far more likely to listen to your article idea with a friendly ear.

For a really complete media contact file, a standard phone file card is probably not going to be large enough to accommodate all the information you will want to include. You may prefer to use large file cards or even a three-ring notebook with individual sheets for each specific medium and alphabet tabs to make finding the specific medium you're looking for easier.

WHAT GOES IN YOUR MEDIA FILE

A basic individual media contact file should include:

1. The name, location, and mailing address (including ZIP) of the medium.

2. The particulars of that medium: for instance, the exact hours and days of a radio or TV station's newscasts; or whether the newspaper is a daily or weekly, whether it publishes evenings or mornings, whether or not it has a Sunday edition.

3. The medium's area of influence. For most media this will be defined in terms of geography—the daily newspaper covers these specific counties; the TV station goes out to a radius of so many miles. But for other media the influence area may be defined in terms of demographics or life-style, as, for instance, a newsletter for retirees or a local magazine directed at an upscale audience segment.

4. A list of the medium's deadlines.

5. The medium's master switchboard phone number. In addition, most media have numbers that ring directly into the newsroom.

6. The names and direct phone line numbers of key personnel—the editor-in-chief, the city or metro editor, the news director, the assignment editor, the public affairs director, and specific reporters you know who specialize in your type of material, for instance, the business reporter or a feature writer. Such people tend to move around a lot, so it's especially important to keep this section of your media file up-to-date.

7. Other specialized information that might be of particular interest to you, such as:

- A list of once-a-year special sections of the newspaper pertinent to your business. For example, if you operate a bridal shop you should be especially interested in the spring bridal section usually published in February. Note not only when they are published, but the deadlines for ads and/or editorial copy. Include the names of writers and/or editors who work on the section.
- A rundown of public service shows carried by the electronic media. Include the day of the week and time they are generally aired, the name of the host and producer (sometimes it's the same person, usually it's not), and booking deadlines.

Also be careful to watch for any themes these public service shows seem to favor. For example, one show may tend to specialize in family-oriented subjects, another in education or health-related topics.

- Info on whether they carry public service announcements (PSAs), how you can qualify, and who is responsible for scheduling them.
- A list of the hot topics the media, either electronic or print, appear to be paying attention to. Sometimes these are strictly local, sometimes they reflect national trends. For example, for much of the mid-1980s entrepreneurs seemed to be the darlings of the media. If you can relate your release to one of these hot topics, it very much enhances your chances of getting some ink or airtime.

8. A log of the subjects and dates of news releases you have sent and of the personal contacts you have made at a particular medium.

9. A log of the subjects, lengths (in column inches or minutes), and dates published or broadcast of stories about your business, agency, or group used by that medium. Be sure to note where each story was used, such as in a special section of the paper or on a regular newscast. Also note whether the story idea was initiated by the media or was generated as the result of a news release or personal contact with you.

10. A copy of that medium's ad rate card, from which you can calculate the "value" of the coverage you have received on the basis of what it would have cost if you had been obliged to pay for it. You may be pleasantly surprised at the end of the year to find just how much money you have "saved."

Sample media files can be seen in Figures 11–1, 11–2, and 11–3.

(text continued on page 136)

Figure 11-1. Sample media file for a local daily newspaper kept by a local retailer of lawn and garden supplies and equipment.

Suburba Herald   (999)555—1212
101 Main St. / PO Box 23   (switchboard)
Suburba, Idaho 11111

Evening, Monday through Friday
Morning, Saturday and Sunday

Paid circulation—19,800 daily, 28,500 Sunday, in Suburba and 10 miles north and west into rural area; 95% carrier delivery. Suburba pop., 55,000; total in area served by *Herald*, 105,000.

Combo ad buys with *Westside Times* and *North Shore News;* no combo on editorial material.

Deadlines:

- 9 A.M. weekdays for local page.
- 3 P.M. Friday for Sat. A.M. local page.
- Noon Wednesday for Sunday feature sections.
- Special sections of interest to us:
- Year-end ("Progress") issued last Sunday in January; article ideas due by mid-Nov., copy due about Dec. 1.
- Spring Lawn and Garden issued 2nd or 3rd week in February; article ideas due about Jan. 1; final copy due Feb. 1.
- Fall Lawn and Garden issued first Sunday after Labor Day; ideas due by July 15, final copy by Aug. 1.

Contacts:
- Ron Jenkins, publisher: 555—1213 (direct); Ruth Gorman his Secy., a member of our church.
- Bill Travers, editor: 555—1215 (direct).
- Joan "Sissy" Madison, city editor: 555—1217.
- Bob Barstow, feature editor: 555—1218.
- Eleanor Scott, copy editor: 555—1219; her son plays on baseball team with our son.
- Bob or Eleanor handle most special sections.

(continued)

Figure 11-1 *(continued)*

Offset press—Can use glossy B&W prints and color slides; ad slicks
and line art also OK.

What they've used:

1. Did city page feature on Sally and me in connection with our
   grand opening, March 1985. From our release. They took
   pictures of us and equipment. Total, 24 col. inches (@ $13/
   col. in. = $312).
2. Used how-to piece on lawn feeding in Fall L&G section,
   1985; I rewrote from extension service handout with my
   byline; photo of our equipment; total, 15.5 col. inches (@
   $13/col. in. = $201.50).
3. Used weed control article we rewrote from Scott's literature
   in Spring L&G section, 1986; photo composite of weed types
   from Scott; total, 21 col. inches (@ $13 per = $273).
4. Business page brief, May 1986, when we announced we
   would be open Sunday afternoons, May 15 through Oct. 15;
   total 3.5 col. inches (@ $13/= $45.50).
5. Business page brief, Nov. 1986, when we promoted George
   to service shop manager; total, 4.5 inches ($67.50).
6. How-to article on safe/correct way to mow slopes in Spring
   L&G section, 1987; interview based on my suggestion to B.
   Barstow; three photos (one in color) we helped set up; total,
   30 col. inches ($450).
7. City page photo of Sally and neighborhood kids we organized
   as part of citywide cleanup day, April 1987; 10 col. inches
   (@ $15/= $130).
8. Page one photo of mayor, Sally, & me at ground breaking for
   our greenhouse as part of expansion into landscaping, Sept.
   1987; story inside on city page, also with photos of staff and
   customers; total, 26 col. inches ($390).

Figure 11 -2.   Sample media file for a local TV station kept by the volunteer publicity chairperson of a local Strawberry Festival.

WYXZ-TV (Channel 6)   (999) 555–9876
3rd & Main Sts.   (main switchboard)
Ourtown, Tennessee 98765   8:30 to 5:30 weekdays and 8–12 Sat.
                             555–9880 (newsroom, after hours)

7 P.M. & 11 P.M.—30-min. news, Mon. thru Fri.
6:30 P.M. & 11 P.M.—30-min. news, Sat.
11 P.M.—30-min news, Sun.
5-min. "updates" at 6:45 & 7:45 A.M., weekdays

News will use live on-camera interview of newsmaker when they
    have solicited it; will rarely accept outside offer.
News will *only* use tape they've produced, but will sometimes accept
    slides.

"Focus on Ourtown"—30-min. weekly public affairs show, broadcast
    various times Sunday A.M. Usually two topics per show, approx.
    15 min. each; one or two guests per topic; sometimes entire
    program on one topic; topics always local.
"Business Perspective"—30 min. once a month public affairs show
    in coop. with Chamber of Commerce. Broadcast twice during
    month, usually after midnight on a weekday. Usually includes
    taped on-site interviews with chamber exec. and one or more
    local businesses.
"Education Perspective"—same format as "Bus. Persp." but does
    school supt. and staff, including local community college.
Community Calendar: 30-sec. to 1-min. spots run at various times
    with brief promos, 10 to 12 seconds each, of upcoming events
    in Ourtown area.

Public service shows will use good-quality VHS tapes at their discre-
    tion; will use slides and in-studio demonstrations.

Channel 6 covers all of Jefferson, Washington, and Lincoln counties
    and portions of Madison, VanBuren, Grant, Taylor, and Bu-
    chanan counties. Total pop. covered, about 165,000; Ourtown
    pop., 85,000.

(continued)

Figure 11-2 (*continued*)

Deadlines:

- Weekday early news, 4 P.M.
- Weekday late news, 7 P.M.
- Weekend early news, 2 P.M.
- Weekend late news, 5 P.M. These are for last-minute hand delivery.
- 48 hours notice required for scheduling nonemergency news conference.
- "Focus" topic *proposals*—at least 90 days before broadcast; taping usually 3 to 4 weeks prior to broadcast.
- "Perspective" topic *proposals*—6 months prior to broadcast; tape 4 to 6 weeks ahead.
- Calendar—45 to 60 days ahead of event.

Contacts:

- John L. Grogan, Gen. Mgr.: 555–9878; Kay Vance, secy.
- Becky Simmons, News Dir.: 555–9879; new last year, from Green Bay, Wis.
- Sam Williams, Assign. Edit.: 555–9880; former reporter, moved up when Becky came in.
- Tammy Villanova, Public Affairs Dir., "Focus" producer and host: 555–9882; doing show for at least 5 years; met her at many Chamber of Commerce events.
- Shawn Tipton, Tammy's asst.: 555–9882; "Perspective" producer and coordinates most calendar items; new, first job in TV.
- Bruce Benson, reporter: 555–9880, sometimes produces "Focus" and "Perspective" shows.

What they've used on Strawberry Festival:

Prior to 1/86 no notes or records kept; this summary based on recollections of former publicity chair and other board members:

1. For years 1968 (first festival) through 1978—ran community calendar announcements; varied as to how many times each year; this was *only* TV promo of event. They have con-

tinued to run community calendar announcements each year since.
2. Possibly a public service show appearance the first year.
3. News department covered the festival "a couple" of times during these years; which years not determinable.
4. In 1979—began annual appearances on public service show; in 1983 or '84—began using slides from previous year's festival.
5. Starting '80 or '81—news department covered festival on annual basis, usually with tape clip of opening day.

After 1/86:

1. 3/86—entire "Focus" on festival, including live demonstration of cooking with strawberries; @ $150/minute, $4500.
2. 3/86—community college marketing class produced 30-sec. spot in lab for festival; Ch. 6, others, run as PSA 8 times 5/86 and 6/86; about $1800.
3. 6/86—hold first news conference to announce candidates for festival beauty queen; Ch. 6 gave it 1.5 min. on early news, 1 min. on late news; $375.
4. 6/86—Ch. 6 news coverage of festival: Opening day ceremonies, 2 min. early, same late; $300. Kids' strawberry costume contest, 2nd day, 1.75 min. early news, 45 sec. late; $375.
5. 8/86—cover check presentation from festival profits to sheltered workshop; 25 sec. on early news, none on late news; $100.
6. 11/86—5-min. segment on "Perspective Schools" of volunteer from festival giving elementary class nutrition info on strawberries; $750.
7. 1986 total, $8200.
8. 1/87—cover news conference; introduce festival's new clown mascot, "Strawberry Kid," 60 sec. both early and late news; $300.

Figure 11-3. Sample media file for a local news/talk
radio station kept by a new architectural firm specializing
in restoration and renovation of old or historic buildings.

KLMN-AM   (818) 555-6676
300 First Bank Building   weekdays, 8 to 5
PO Box 33   555-6678 (newsroom)
Anytown, Wisconsin 98765   555-TALK (talk show)

Local newscasts

- 5 min. at 2:55, 4:55, 7:55, 8:55, and 10:55 A.M.; 1:55, 3:55,
  6:55, 8:55, and 10:55 P.M.
- 15 min. at 6:15 A.M., 12:15, and 5:15 P.M.

Local phone-in talk shows

- Jason Bond, weekdays 9 to 11 A.M., general topics and current issues, uses a lot of guests.
- Carolee Best, weekdays 1 to 3:30 P.M., health, nutrition, and
  family topics, limited guests.
- Joe Greene, Sat., 9 to 11 A.M., home and auto how-to and fixit
  tips, uses a lot of guests.
- Mike Fast, Sun., 7 to 9 P.M., all sports.

Other public service

- Weekly 15-min. prerecorded interviews on specific current
  topics, run four to five times per week at varying hours.
- 5-min. community calendar with that day's events (10 to 15
  sec. each), seven days a week at 5:55 and 6:55 A.M.
- Some items from comm. cal. also run as individual PSAs during day.

Range—about 30 mi. around Anytown, 45,000 tot. pop.

Deadlines:

- News releases—one business day prior to release.
- Phone-in talk shows—topics & guests normally booked 14 to
  21 days prior to appearance; always subject to last-minute
  change.

- Interview topics and guests booked 8 to 12 weeks in advance; some weeks reserved 6 to 8 months ahead.
- Community calendar & PSAs—one week ahead of run date.

Contacts:

- Alex Brown, station GM: 555–6776; Mark went to school with Alex.
- Ron Hall, News Dir.: 555–6778.
- Sandra Wilson, producer, and Wendy Williams, assoc. producer, for Jason Bond and Carolee Best: 555–6676.
- Joe Greene, produces own show: 555–6776; also contact him at his lumber yard: 555–7654; Joe is Jim's brother-in-law.
- Fred Strickland, Public Affairs Director: 555–6776; produces interview show; Jan White, secy., coordinates community calendar items.

What they've used:

1. 3/87—Mark did 15-min. interview show as new chairman of county historical society, mentioning plans to restore old church building as local history museum (@ $35/min. = $525).
2. 6/87—Jim did 30-min. guest shot on Carolee Best talk show about how kitchens have changed since Anytown founded in 1850s (@ $35/ = $1050).
3. 11/87—Jim guest on Joe Greene show, answering questions on do-it-yourself restoration projects (@ $35/ = $4200).
4. 1/88—Mark quoted as part of news coverage of news conference announcing fund drive for local history museum (@ $35/ = $20).
5. 2/88—Mark quoted as part of news coverage of fund drive progress report ($20?).
6. 3/88—Mark mentioned in station's editorial in support of fund drive ($20?).
7. 4/88—Mark quoted when $ goal reached ($20?).

WHY TRACK THE MEDIA?

At first glance, it may sound like a lot of busywork—measuring and recording the column inches of newspaper or magazine articles and the airtime in minutes and seconds of stories about your business, agency, or group. For many groups this may not be necessary at all: Just the most basic tracking system may be enough.

But you should at least be aware that many businesses and agencies, even small ones, do carefully track not only coverage of themselves but also coverage of their competitors and of key issues in their industry. Why go to all that work?

First, tracking coverage of others in your field is a good way to gather competitor intelligence. For example, what would it tell you if another independently owned pharmacy across town was suddenly featured on the local business page because of a large showroom/warehouse addition it was going to build?

Second, tracking the coverage local media give to general issues that are important to you can potentially lead to all sorts of benefits—from spotting a hot new consumer fad that allows you to order a product and have it on your shelves well ahead of your competition to identifying shifts in public attitudes that help you get the ear of legislators or regulators who impact on your agency or group.

John Naisbitt's best-selling book *Megatrends* and his popular "Trendletter" newsletter are both based on detailed tracking of numerous issues and topics covered in the national and local media across the country.

Third, by carefully tracking the equivalent paid advertising dollar value of the editorial exposure you're able to generate, you may discover that you can switch some of your paid ad budget to publicity efforts. Indeed, you may even find that you can reduce your overall promotion budget and still maintain the same effectiveness by making more extensive use of "free" publicity.

Don't Ignore the Little Media

A reminder. . . . Don't focus all your attention on just the so-called major media in your market—the network-affiliated TV stations and daily newspapers—in building your media contact list. Remember, the competition for exposure in the major media is intense. And, if you'll recall, one of their fundamental weaknesses is the shotgun effect. While they do indeed reach large numbers of people, sometimes those large numbers don't include the specific target audience you want or need to reach.

Conversely, there may be smaller, more specialized media in your market that not only reach the people you specifically want to reach but, even more important, are also far more amenable to carrying your stories and articles than the major media.

SOURCES FOR BUILDING YOUR MEDIA FILE

Of course you start with the local media you're personally aware of—the daily or weekly newspaper(s) you subscribe to, the TV and radio stations based in your community or that serve your area. These will probably represent the major local media, that is, how most people in your community get their local news and information.

Start with the local phone book to get their phone numbers and addresses.

Look in the yellow pages of the directory under various headings—newspapers, broadcasters, television—to find other media that may not immediately come to mind, like the rock'n'roll station (or classical music station) you never listen to!

When you have a complete basic list of the major media, start filling in the details. Call the TV and radio stations and ask for the name and phone number of the news director and assignment editor. Call the newspaper and ask for the name and number of the managing editor, the city editor, the business editor, and perhaps the features editor.

Then go on to ask for the other information you need to know, like deadlines for news stories and PSAs, production requirements, subjects and dates of any special sections of the paper, and so on. You want your list to be as complete as possible.

Next, start scouring the area for the little media, the ones that serve specialty markets. I can almost guarantee that you're going to be surprised at how many you uncover.

What about the opposite side of that coin? Should you include nonlocal media in your contact file? The answer is a qualified "yes."

As I said in the introduction, one of my basic assumptions is that you are a small business, agency, or organization whose principal interest is in generating publicity at the local level. You're not looking for a guest appearance on the "Phil Donahue Show" or a cover story in *Time*. So I will not suggest that you add the name of the producer of the Donahue show to your list.

However, you should be more or less routinely sending your news releases to the trade publications in your industry. These should definitely be included in your media contact file.

Getting Started Tomorrow Morning

Get a three-ring notebook and some lined paper or a pack of 5 x 7 lined index cards. At the top of each page or card, write the name of an individual medium—newspaper, broadcast station, trade journal. List all those that are located in or that serve your market. Look up their addresses and phone numbers in the phone book.

Ask your employees, coworkers, and friends to write down a list of the names of the media they watch, listen to, and read. Especially encourage them to list the little publications they read. Then add media to your list from theirs as appropriate, and do the same thing by either formally or informally surveying your customers, clients, or members.

Do what I call a "walk around survey." That is, as you're going about your daily activities, take note of the various publications that you can just pick up from stacks in restaurants, supermarkets, drugstores, and on the street. Add any that are appropriate to your media list.

Do a "piled on the filing cabinet survey." That is, check the titles of the various trade publications that arrive in your office by mail and get piled on the filing cabinet to be read later when you have time. Add these to your media list.

Finally, go to your local library's reference section and check the publications directories it has on its shelves. Again, you'll probably be surprised at how many there are. These directories are a good place in which to find those more obscure trade publications, and to get more detailed information on your local media. Here are a few of the standard directories almost all libraries carry:

- *The Gale Directory of Publications* (formerly the *Ayer Directory*) lists the names, addresses, and phone numbers of almost all news-papers, weekly as well as daily, and magazines published in the United States and Canada.
- *Broadcasting/Cablecasting Yearbook* is *the* reference source in which to find the call letters, addresses, phone numbers, and other pertinent info—such as if the radio station is a Top-40 or news/talk format—on TV and radio stations and cable systems.
- *Editor & Publisher Yearbook* gives you the names of the editors and top reporters for virtually every newspaper in the country, plus addresses and phones.
- *Standard Rate & Data* is the advertising industry's standard reference because it gives circulation figures and advertising rate data.

12

Planning for Good Publicity

In the preceding chapters, I've offered literally hundreds of specific tips and dozens and dozens of action suggestions on how you can generate more positive publicity for your business, agency, or group. Now it's time to think about how you can keep all those projects organized and on track. We need to talk about *planning* your publicity programs.

To pick up on the analogy introduced in earlier chapters, if the news release is the basic tool of public relations, as the carpenter's hammer and saw are of his trade, and you can build a basic public relations program just by using news releases, just as a carpenter can build a basic shelter with only a hammer and saw. . . .

Then it's possible for you to send out news releases as the ideas occur to you and when you have time, but without much advance planning, just as it's theoretically possible for a carpenter to build an acceptable shelter out of his head, without using any plans, blueprints, or drawings.

But, in either case, you'll get a much better publicity program, and a much better house, if you have a plan to work from.

Big corporations' annual marketing, public relations, and publicity plans fill entire notebooks. Yours probably won't be that sophisticated. Nor does it have to be.

But before you actually start writing a publicity plan, there are a few tangents I want to go off on briefly. In fact, they've been a kind of undercurrent throughout this book. Now, to stress their importance, I want to take a look at them as stand-alone topics in this chapter.

IMAGE: WHO AND WHAT YOU ARE

The first topic is image. It's a real buzzword in public relations, often used by outsiders in a deprecating way: "Oh, those PR flacks are just trying to polish up that sleazebag's image." Unfortunately, there are times when public relations departments are, indeed, called upon to try to refurbish a lost reputation or tarnished image.

Hopefully, that's not why you'll be thinking about news releases and publicity programs. As I've tried to suggest a number of times, your publicity program should be proactive and stress the positive.

In fact, because of the somewhat negative image "image" has acquired in the popular media, that's why up to now I've avoided using that specific word. Yet, in the final analysis, that's precisely what public relations and publicity are all about: *your* organization's effort at getting people out there—your customers, clients, contributors, constituents, community leaders, professional colleagues, stockholders, potential investors, employees and potential employees, friends, and neighbors—who read articles about you or who see you on TV to have a positive perception of who you are.

Remember, I said that there are always certain assumptions made about the audience and its information needs whenever an author sits down to write a book. In the same way, every time you sit down to write a news release or design a media kit or develop a special feature story idea, you consciously or unconsciously make assumptions about your image, about who you are!

And that's the key question: Who are you? That's the question you have to ask yourself *consciously* before you start to develop your overall publicity plan, as well as each time you sit down at the typewriter or word processor to knock out another news release. The more specifically you can answer this question, the better. Why?

First, because you want to continually build and reinforce the same positive image about yourself. For example, in your town there are probably places like *the* men's store or *the* restaurant or *the* business luncheon club. There may be other men's stores or restaurants or business luncheon clubs, but these have, over time, built a consistent image that makes them the leaders in their respective fields. You want to be *the* business in your field, or *the* professional service in your area, or *the* human service or health agency, or *the* volunteer organization.

Second, and in the same vein, because you don't want any contradictory or conflicting images or perceptions about you to arise. All this will do is confuse the community and weaken your image. For instance, if you're an old established business that's been on the decline for several years, but you've just been taken over by a new and aggressive young management team, you would want *either* to stress the changes and vitality of the "new" company or to emphasize the continuity with the past. You have to be one or the other, you can't be both.

Third, because you may very well want to change an existing image. How do you expect to know what you're changing *to* if you don't know what it is that you're changing *from*?

Saying something vague and general like "We're a men's retail clothing store" simply isn't enough. There are lots of "men's retail clothing stores" around. How is yours different? Are you an upscale men's clothing store or a working man's shop? Do you deal in traditional styles or specialize in current high-fashion looks? Are you price-driven or personal service-oriented? Are you an old established store with decades of reputation or are you a brand-new shop?

If you're a price-oriented, working man's, blue jeans type of shop, the tone of your news release will be very different from the one you would write if you specialized in $500 suits for professionals and executives. And it will also have a significant impact on which media you send it to.

AUDIENCE: THE PEOPLE YOU WANT TO REACH

The second topic is, in effect, the other side of the same coin. That is, you must also give some thought to your audience. Who are you writing your news release for? Who do you want to read it? The jargon term for this exercise among public relations professionals is targeting.

Even though the major media—newspapers, TV, radio—tend to have large, undifferentiated audiences, by the tone you write in and the things you choose to emphasize, you are to some degree selecting your audience. Certainly how the media choose to play your item, which you can't control directly, can also have an impact on which audience segments pay attention and which don't.

But knowing as much as you can about who you are writing for is an especially important question you must give conscious thought to when you deal with the specialty or nonmajor media, since their whole approach is based on serving the specialized needs of specific audience groups.

For example, say you are a plastics engineer about to write a news release announcing the names of those who have been elected next year's officers of the local Professional Plastics Engineers Society. Your audience for this release will be very different from the audience you would be writing for if you were about to announce that you'd just received a patent on a new plastic compound that's stronger than steel, but lighter than aluminum, and that will probably revolutionize the auto body industry!

The answers to these questions about your image and your intended audience can and should have an impact on what you write, the style and approach you take, even the media you select to send your news releases to.

ETHICS AND TRUST

The third area that needs to be mentioned specifically—trust—has certainly been implied numerous times throughout this book. Yet I simply cannot overstate the importance of carefully developing, nurturing, and protecting a relationship of trust and respect with the media! You can be the finest writer in two counties; you can always have the most gee whiz news items to tell; you can have really wonderful visuals for the TV people every time you hold a news conference. . . . But these won't mean a thing if the media have no faith in the accuracy and news value of your information. Without that trust and respect, your "great" writing, if used at all, will get edited to the point of unrecognizability, your gee whiz story ideas will be buried next to the hog markets, and your news conferences will be sparsely attended, if at all!

Yes, some "PR types" have acquired a less than ideal reputation for their supposed willingness to play fast and loose with the truth at times, for too often churning out news releases that are little more than meaningless fluff, and for sometimes engaging in questionable ethical gymnastics in order to enhance or protect their clients' or company's image. Maybe they can even get away with this kind of activity for a while, especially if they are fast on their feet and can, so to speak, "kite their checks" with the media by dealing with different media in different parts of the country or by jumping around from various national media to trade publications.

But when you're dealing with local media day in and day out, when the editor of the paper's daughter might be in the same middle school class as your son, when the TV reporter who handles most of the business stories might be a member of your church, when you bump into the general manager of the local radio station all the time at the chamber of commerce legislative committee, then you simply cannot afford to be thought of as one of those PR types who can't be trusted.

When you're announcing a news conference, never overplay the importance of the announcement in the hope that you'll get the media to cover something that really isn't worth covering. You may sucker the media once, but I guarantee it'll be only once.

If you promise the media you'll deliver an article or a media kit or a photo by a certain deadline, scrupulously meet that deadline. The same holds for keeping and being on time for appointments with editors, news directors, even "lowly" reporters.

Don't "fluff" news releases. "Fluffing" means padding a news release with overly wordy quotations that don't get to the point or with lengthy "mood" descriptions of people or buildings or places. Like those K-9 patrol dogs trained to sniff out drugs, editors, news directors, and reporters have an extremely sensitive nose for smelling out fluff and will be unmerciful with the delete key on their terminal when it comes to slicing a fluffed news release down to size!

Finally, although I've said this more than once in the section on dealing with the media in crisis situations, it bears repeating:

Never, never deceive—lie to—the media. Period! It is *the* cardinal sin in your relationship with the media. They can overlook some occasional fluffing and even ignore your giving some other media a better story every once in a while. But they are a long, long time—if ever!—forgiving you for not telling them the truth.

RESOURCES: YOUR BASIC REQUIREMENTS

Finally, there is one more crucial question you have to ask yourself before you can really get rolling on developing your publicity plan: What do you have to work with? Here's a checklist of important items that you can use to develop an inventory of your resources.

1. You need a good typewriter or word processor with letter-quality printer. You do *not* submit handwritten press releases. But *no* dot matrix printers, please. In the eyes of a busy editor, dot matrix printers are only just barely above handwriting. In fact, many magazines that take free-lance material specify that they will not even read dot matrix manuscripts.

2. Access to a copying machine is a must. Even the smallest community is going to have at least a half dozen media, and most communities will have more—too many to make retyping the release that many times, or even trying multiple carbons, practicable.

3. You will of course need a postage meter or large supply of stamps, since, as I suggested, 99 percent of your news releases will be delivered by mail.

4. You need to have access to a photographer who knows how to handle a 35mm camera. Although I did suggest that in most cases the media prefer to shoot their own photographs, sooner or later you're going to want to include some pictures of your own with your news release or media kit.

If you're lucky—very lucky!—your brother-in-law can, in fact, handle a camera and will deliver a near-professional-quality photograph. Unfortunately, most of the time these all-too-willing volunteers have no idea how to compose or light a photo for publication purposes, so that what you get are gray, slightly out-of-focus prints of stiffly posed subjects. You get the picture, or, rather, you *don't* get the picture.

Before you assign *any* photographer, professional or amateur, to shoot for you, look at what he or she has done before. It should include camera work for publication. The photographer may have shot some of the most breathtaking scenic vistas you've ever seen, but that still doesn't mean he or she knows how to take the kind of basic pictures that a newspaper or magazine will use.

5. You need access to film processing facilities. You may have a darkroom, your photographer may have his or her own, or you might have to use a professional lab.

I do not recommend taking your black and white film to the corner drugstore for processing—for several reasons:

First, most of these people use commercial processing labs that are almost totally geared for color prints or slide work. So when you hand them a roll of black and white, they're likely to look at it as if it were a strange object from outer space.

Second, because their regular labs specialize in color work, they have to send it to a special lab. This means it doesn't fit their normal pickup and delivery schedule, so it usually takes a week or more for you to get your prints back.

Third, and most important, most of these labs use automated film-processing machines. There is little, if any, effort made to compensate for mistakes that were made or were unavoidable. In other words, the quality of the prints is usually not what it could or should be, especially for publication purposes.

Instead, I suggest using a custom photo processing lab, where they develop the film and make prints by hand. They will take the time and effort to compensate for less than ideal shooting conditions. Most larger cities have at least one custom lab. It'll cost a bit more, but the superior results are worth it—you'll be much more likely to see your photo in the paper or magazine!

6. You'll need plenty of letterhead stationery on which to type your news releases and imprint envelopes in which to send them. Should you have a special letterhead just for your news release? While PR agencies and larger corporate PR departments use them, for most small businesses, agencies, or groups this is probably not necessary.

7. You need to have a telephone answered at all times or hooked up to an answering machine (which, of course, should be checked frequently). This is in case the media need to clarify a fact on a news release, or, better yet, want to schedule a follow-up interview.

8. You of course need your media file—a notebook, a 5 × 7 card file, or, if you're lucky, a computer.

9. You'll also need a contact file for resources other than media. A Rolodex or address book right next to the telephone is perfect for this.

10. For conducting interviews, taking notes at lectures, jotting down ideas for news releases, and other purposes, you'll need a supply of stenopads or reporter's notebooks, which are just mini-versions of the stenopad. Any good office supply store stocks these items. And if you can afford it, a mini tape recorder for interviews and verbal notes is a great convenience.

11. You'll need the usual inventory of office supplies—pencils, pens, paper clips, tape, scissors, ruler, stapler and staple remover, a sponge for wetting stamps and sealing envelopes, and phone message pads or scratch pads.

12. Eventually, you are sure to need a filing cabinet and file folders. As your publicity program progresses, you'll generate numerous files—projects in process files, future project files, files for copies of old news releases, files for copies of notes from past releases, files of other publicists' good ideas, and so on.

13. You need a work space, ideally a desk or work table where you can set up your material and leave it. For some volunteer groups, the kitchen table or a card table temporarily set up in the family room may, by necessity, have to suffice.

14. If you have only one book sitting on your desk, make it a good dictionary! The old rule of thumb is as true as it's always been: If in doubt about a word's spelling or meaning, check it. Or, if you love gadgets, and can afford it, there are some excellent electronic dictionaries on the market.

15. To keep you in the journalistic mainstream, you should also have a stylebook. Stylebooks are published by the media to give their reporters clear and consistent guidelines on the writing

formats and practices that are unique to the journalism field and that are generally not covered in traditional style manuals.

If you're serious about developing your publicity program, you should acquire and study a stylebook. There are a number on the market, so ask at any good general bookstore what is in stock, or check your local library.

16. A thesaurus will help you to find "just the right word" and is almost as useful as a dictionary.

17. You're going to need either a manual or computer-based system for maintaining mailing labels, including your media lists and any other lists you may develop.

If you're lucky, you can keep it on a computer. If you don't have access to a computer, stop in at any good office supply store and check out the various manual systems there are for doing mailing labels on the typewriter.

18. There may be an occasion when you will need to have a graphic artist or computer graphics person develop graphs or charts or maps for a press release.

19. Naturally you'll need a subscription to the paper or papers in your area and to other appropriate publications, such as trade journals, so that you can see what they do with your material.

20. You'll want an AM/FM radio so that you can monitor their coverage.

21. And you'll want a TV so that you can monitor news and public service shows-and a VCR to record those of particular interest to you.

Do you have access to these things? Which of these resources are available in house, and which do you have to go outside for?

Although a not-for-profit agency or a volunteer group can usually ask for various kinds of work *pro bono* (without charge), small businesses may be uncomfortable asking for freebies.

However, there are many kinds of services available to small businesses at relatively little cost. For example, many technical and community colleges have computer labs with very sophisticated graphics or desktop publishing programs, and they might be willing to do an occasional graph or chart for you at a minimal cost as a lab experience for their students.

There are also many one- and two-person free-lance desktop publishing shops springing up that will do a single project at a very reasonable cost.

What "in kind" services are available from volunteers or staff? This is a variation of the above, but purely from the standpoint of the nonprofit agency or volunteer group.

As the volunteer PR person for a human services agency, you may not have a computer of your own, but during off hours— evenings and weekends—you may have access to the one the agency uses.

Or, as the volunteer publicity person for a local model railroad club, you may not have a typewriter, but one of your members volunteers the use of his secretary on occasion to type news releases for you.

How much hard cash do you have to spend? What's your budget? How does the publicity budget fit in with other promotional expenses, like advertising or direct mail? This is an important question, because the answer for a small business may be very different than for a volunteer club.

Small businesses will want to know what kinds of "canned" news releases, product photos, brochures, or other background materials are available from manufacturers and suppliers and in what quantities. Health or human services agencies might ask a similar question of their national affiliates or professional organizations.

Whether you're doing publicity for a small business, agency, or club, if it's been around for a number of years you should find out what kinds of historic data—old photos, scrapbooks, diaries, documents, artifacts—might be available. As suggested earlier, this kind of material often makes an excellent feature story.

BASIC PLANNING APPROACHES

Both the overall structure of a publicity plan and the specific details of it are so dependent on individual situations that it's not easy to provide you with solid advice. However, there are a couple of basic approaches to publicity planning that, while not ideal in all situations, will work reasonably well for most small businesses, agencies, or groups.

Probably the most common approach to publicity planning is to base it on some fixed event (or events) and then to time your news releases and media activities accordingly. For example:

• A church is going to celebrate its hundredth anniversary. The publicity committee would start with the date of the celebration and then work backward to build its plan, plugging in dates for news conferences, sending out news releases and media kits, getting a special feature story in the newspaper, making appearances on TV public service shows and radio talk shows, possibly starting as much as a full year in advance.

• A ski resort business is highly seasonal. It would probably want to plan for most of its publicity and news releases to appear during the months when people are either thinking about winter vacations or actually on vacation, and not place much emphasis on the off-season. Its plan would reflect this emphasis, with preparatory activities, such as researching article ideas dominating the early stages, then building to a crescendo as the season draws near.

• A health services agency is going to announce a major new service. It would want to carefully plan its news releases and/or news conference so that the announcements in the various media—TV, radio, local newspapers, industry newsletters—all break at exactly the same time. In this case, to let the word out piecemeal would be a mistake, because the agency wants the maximum exposure for itself and does not want to tip its hand to the competition. Its publicity plan for this one event might encompass only a few months.

A variation of this approach would be for your group, agency, or small business to set a goal of generating a minimum number of media exposures—each defined as a nonpaid appearance in at least one medium—over a given period of time:

• A newly opened accounting and tax preparation service might set the goal of a minimum of six nonpaid local media exposures during the first year, with at least three of them being in print and three on electronic media.

• A long-established local civic club that's experiencing a slow decline in membership might decide to target young professionals for membership and for that purpose develop the goal of securing at least one positive mention of the club in each of the five journals read by local professionals during the next six months.

• A small college is planning to launch a capital fund drive in eighteen to twenty-four months. It may set a goal of generating some kind of favorable news release or letter to the editor or guest appearance on a TV or radio talk show at least once every two months between now and then. It may even go a step further and specify that in each of these media appearances one of the following themes will be stressed: how much the college has grown over the past quarter century, how it has "made do" with no new buildings for more than twenty years, how technology-intensive tomorrow's educational needs will be, and how badly the college needs a new science and computer technology building.

Some ideas for news releases will fall into place on the calendar rather quickly, like the annual community open house your agency always holds in April or the annual anniversary sale your shop holds each fall.

Some may be the result of opportunities that you can't control but that you could typically expect to occur at some time during the year, such as staff changes.

Still others you may have to consciously develop to fill gaps in the calendar in order to meet your goal.

Setting up specific publicity goals for your small business, agency, or group forces you to carefully watch what's going on in your organization and to be constantly thinking about news release and/or feature story ideas. In the end, you may not follow the plan religiously, but if you do have some form of plan, I can almost guarantee that you will get more media coverage than you've ever had in the past.

ONE BIG STORY OR LOTS OF LITTLE ONES?

The question almost always comes up: Should I try for one or two big stories a year, or should I send out lots of little, more or less routine releases and go for frequency of appearance? In virtually ninety-nine cases out of a hundred, my recommendation would be to follow the latter strategy, that is, emphasize frequency and regularity over the one big impact. Here's why:

• It's simply a lot easier to get a couple of inches of space in the newspaper or twenty seconds or so of airtime than it is to get a thirty-two-inch feature story in the paper or a two-minute in-depth report on TV. Editors and news directors tend to guard their most valuable commodity—space and airtime—jealously. They're not giving away much if it's "only" an inch or two or fifteen or twenty seconds, but it's a lot when you realize that a thirty-two-inch story is close to half a page for most newspapers and that a two-minute report amounts to nearly a tenth of the available newshole for a typical thirty-minute newscast.

• The truth is—as I suggested earlier—that the media prefer to develop their own big stories or story ideas. Again, by running your short, more or less routine release, editors or news directors won't feel as if they are surrendering too much control. However, if they accept your major feature story idea or run your lengthy news release, they have to a certain degree turned over to you some of the control of their product.

• The more times you appear, regardless of how big or small the space or time allotted you, the more you increase your chances of being seen. In the paid advertising field, they call this "buying frequency," and it's the reason you often see the exact same fast food ad or beer commercial run several times a night on several different stations, or even the same station. One ad, just like one article, may be missed. But lots of ads, like lots of expo-sures, have a good chance of being noticed.

• Finally, there is a kind of cumulative effect from regularity of media exposure, the impact of each exposure being greater than its size might normally suggest because it is building on the rec-ognition from previous exposures. To use a somewhat hypotheti-cal illustration, let's say you are able to land a thirty-two-inch feature story on the newspaper's business page about your new business and it has a certain impact on the community, which we will assign the arbitrary number of 10. If, on the other hand, you had received four or five brief articles over a six-month period, none of which was more than three or four inches in length, so that the total amount of exposure was about half in terms of space, what I'm suggesting here is that the cumulative effect of those regular and frequent appearances, instead of being only 5, would actually be a 15 or 18, a number significantly higher than that assigned the one "big" story!

A SEVEN-STEP APPROACH TO BUILDING YOUR PUBLICITY PLAN

Remember all those notes and story ideas you've been filing away? Well here's where they come together. Here's a seven-step approach to writing a do-it-yourself publicity plan for your small business, group, or agency (see Figure 12–1 for a simple plan):

1. First, in no more than one hundred words and/or three sentences, write down who you are. Skip the detail and go for the essence. When people hear your name, what do they think of? In other words, what's your image?

2. Next, in not more than 150 words and/or five sentences, describe the groups that are important to you and explain why they are important. Again don't worry about the details, just get the basics down. In other words, who's your audience?

3. Then, in not more than 150 words and/or five sentences, develop three or four general goals you want to accomplish with your publicity program.

4. Now, decide which of the two basic planning approaches—working back from a fixed event or generating publicity over a given period—is best for you. Explain your choice in not more than one hundred words.

5. Next, pick up all those lists of news release and story ideas you've been saving and go over them carefully. You should be seeing the list in a whole new light.

You will probably find yourself saying about some of your ideas, "Wow, that's a natural for TV." "Gee, the newspapers would really jump at this one." About some of your ideas you may find yourself shaking your head, wondering why on earth you ever thought anyone would be interested in them. And you should find yourself wanting to add ideas to the list.

(text continued on page 159)

Figure 12-1. Sample publicity plan for the grand opening of a Davenport, Iowa bed and breakfast facility.

PUBLICITY PLAN

MISSISSIPPI PINES B&B

Who We Are

We are a four guest-room, 125-year-old bed and breakfast inn in Davenport, Iowa. Two things distinguish us from other B&Bs. We are on the edge of a bluff about a quarter mile from the Mississippi River, and all our guest bedrooms, our parlor, and our porch overlook the river. Each afternoon from 4 to 5 p.m., my wife, who is a retired piano teacher and performer, plays a miniconcert for our guests in the parlor.

Our Target Customer Groups

<u>Age and lifestyle</u>—Empty nesters and/or young couples with no small children who are looking for a unique overnight accommodation; people interested in a getaway weekend; people with the time and the affluence.

<u>Geography</u>—Primary group is those who live within a three-hour drive, which includes Des Moines and Cedar Rapids, Iowa; Peoria, Rockford, and the western Chicago suburbs in Illinois; secondary group is within a one-day's drive, which includes the rest of Chicago, Milwaukee, Indianapolis, Detroit, St. Louis, Kansas City, Omaha, and Minneapolis-St. Paul.

Our Goals

1. Get a favorable mention of our name in at least one major medium in the larger urban centers of the primary target area during the three months following our opening.

2. Get favorable mentions of our name in at least two Midwestern regional travel-oriented publications right before or just after our opening.

3. Get as many favorable mentions as we can in other, nonmajor media throughout the primary target market area during our first six months.

4. Get favorable mentions in media in the secondary target market area during our first six months.

Basic Planning Approach

Our grand opening is planned for March or early April of next year, about eight months from now.

Potential Story Ideas in Connection With Our Grand Opening

- A brief history of the 125-year-old house we are converting to a B&B; it was originally built as a steamboat captain's home just before the Civil War.
- A brief description of the unique architectural features and interior decorative elements of the house.
- A brief history of our area and its colorful association with the Mississippi River.
- A rundown of other things to see and do in our area, including historic and scenic attractions, festivals, and other events.
- A brief bio of the owners.
- The announcement of our grand opening ceremony, for which we hope to get two governors to attend, our Iowa governor and the governor of Illinois, as well as some special guests, like a Mark Twain look-alike character and, perhaps, a contingent from our local Civil War reenactment group.
- A backgrounder on how B&Bs got started in Europe and their recent growth in the United States.
- Endorsements and/or testimonials we might receive from well-known personalities, perhaps some of our old friends from the concert circuit.
- Any anecdotes our research may uncover about the house: Was it ever a bordello? Was it on the underground railway during the Civil War?

Some of these articles may be distributed individually, others included in a media kit.

(continued)

Figure 12-1 (*continued*)

Tentative calendar:

AUGUST

- Research history of the house. Get an art or architectural history professor to give us a report; check county records for former owners' names; check local library for local history background, especially if any former owners were prominent locally or elsewhere; check former owners, local library, historical society, local newspaper, others for any unique stories (ghosts?) or old photographs of the house.
- Research media: Get names and addresses of all out-of-town media in our target area, of Midwest regional travel publications, and of B&B publications from directories in the library.
- Get summer exterior photos of building and grounds—flower beds, trees, shady gazebo, river view; both black & white and color slides.
- Start building media file.

SEPTEMBER

- Write or call out-of-town media, ask for name of travel editor, closing dates for any travel planners or special travel sections they do, especially if they are planning any special issues or sections about the Mississippi River and/or our area; ask if they will send a sample issue.
- Begin contacting local media, ask for name of travel editor or whoever handles travel-related material, get info on deadlines, public service shows they do.
- Contact local, regional, or state tourism promotion agencies; find out what they might have planned, especially any travel guides or planners in which we can get editorial coverage; find out if they have any "fam tours" scheduled to our area that we can piggyback on; ask for their recommendations on out-of-market media we might use.
- Continue building media file.

OCTOBER

- Study out-of-town media samples; study other media and/or promotion plans; revise this plan as necessary.

- Begin assembling and outlining facts and info for various stories.
- Gather old photos of home if available.
- Get fall color photos (slides) taken of exterior of building and river view.
- Write to two governors and invite them to grand opening, offering alternative dates.
- Write to local public service show producers to schedule appearances.
- Look up articles about and reviews of other B&Bs in magazines and newspapers to see how they are handled; use as model for our articles?
- Write overview article about our B&B and scheduled opening and send along with photos to Midwest regional travel magazines.

NOVEMBER

- Start writing other articles as outlined above; submit to local tourism agency PR person for critique.
- Contact Mark Twain actor and Civil War group (others?) for grand opening dates; see if they have any photos or other promo stuff to put in advance publicity.
- Continue contacts with media, especially out-of-town media and local public service show hosts.
- Continue building media files.

DECEMBER

- Send overview article and photos to publications (newspapers, tourism promotion agencies) doing spring travel planners.
- Get winter snow shots of building (color and black & white).
- Continue writing and polishing articles.
- Begin assembling tentative media kit, including photos.

JANUARY

- Set final date for grand opening; may depend on two governors' schedules; confirm other guests (Mark Twain, Civil War group).
- Begin making appearances on local public service and/or talk shows.

(continued)

Figure 12-1 (*continued*)

- Begin making appearances on out-of-town talk/public service shows.
- Begin making appearances in print media travel planners.
- Get interior black & white photos and color slides taken.
- Fam tour visits?

FEBRUARY

- Finalize media kit; run off copies of final versions of articles; get photo prints made; begin assembling in pocketed folder.
- Invite special guests to stay with us—old friends from concert circuit, local friends; take photos of them; solicit testimonial letters.
- Confirm grand opening dates with dignitaries; get copies of brief synopsis of their remarks.
- Fam tour visits?

MARCH

- At beginning of month, send out notice of grand opening news conference date at end of March to *all* media, local and out-of-town.
- Make follow-up calls to local media (within 20–25 miles)
- Respond to out-of-town media requests, such as arranging for overnight if they're coming or sending out media kit if not; interviews? color slides? pick up writer or TV crew they're sending?
- News conference and grand opening!

APRIL and beyond

- Send full media kit to all media that did not attend news conference.
- Secure copies of articles, reviews when possible. Get permissions to reprint the most favorable for use as fliers, handouts at shows, inserts in response to requests for information.
- Send letters of invitation to dignitaries (U.S. senators, famous actors or artists with local connections, sports figures) and invite them to stay with us free for one night when they are in town. If they do, get media coverage.
- When we receive any type of award—local beautification, fa-

vorable rating from a guide book, designation as an historic site—
send out news release to all print media within one day's drive and
to regional travel publications.

What should also be emerging is some sense of priority, perhaps even a feeling of urgency. Article Idea A is great, but has to be
in the media before the end of the spring or it loses most of its
impact. Article Idea B is a good one, but it can run almost anytime.

6. Next, take one of those whole-year-on-one-sheet planning
calendars and start to rough out a plan according to which of the
basic planning approaches you have chosen. Write your individual
story ideas on Post-it notes so that you can easily move them
around from month to month or even from week to week as prior-
ities change. You may even want to jot down on those note sheets
which media the idea is most appropriate for and perhaps who in
your organization is responsible for moving that particular project
along.

7. Finally, take all those sheets on which you summarized
your image, audience, and goals and put them along with the
monthly sheets in a three-ring binder. Add your other notes and
publicity project ideas for future reference. That's it. You've got a
basic plan.

It has all the necessary parts of a plan:

- Strategic elements—who you are, your image
- Target markets—your audience
- Goals
- Specific projects
- Who's responsible for the projects

One last warning, however. You're never going to be fully
happy with your plan; you'll always be updating it, revising it, tinkering with it. And that's OK. Publicity and public relations are
essentially creative, dynamic processes. There's no such thing as a
right or wrong answer; there's only what works and what doesn't
work.

If you find something that works, score one for your team. And maybe try it again. If a project doesn't come off quite as you expected, then chalk one up to experience, learn from it, and move on to the next project.

As your experience grows, you'll get better and better at spotting good story ideas, at anticipating what the media will like and use, at writing clear and concise news releases, at making effective appearances on TV and radio talk shows. And you will generate more positive publicity for your small business, agency, or group than you ever thought possible.

APPENDIX

A

Sample News Releases

Seeing how others have handled their news releases, and the different forms they can take, may make working up your own a little easier.

I: TELEDIRECT INTERNATIONAL

TeleDirect International is a Davenport, Iowa-based company that develops and markets computer-aided telemarketing systems based on a highly sophisticated software package it wrote. As with many high-tech firms, much of their early marketing material was technically oriented. The three news releases, with accompanying photos and captions, that follow were used as their first media kit and were written for the purpose of increasing their name identity in the telemarketing hardware/software industry itself, as well as in several industries the company was targeting as markets for its telemarketing system. The kit was sent to local media and to a number of out-of-town trade publications, including two that had specifically asked for background information on TeleDirect International.

There are several things to note as you read these news releases:

• They all carry a "Davenport, Iowa" dateline at the very beginning. This is because the releases were sent to out-of-town media. Releases sent to local media do not need a dateline.

• The first two releases are short, only three pages long, while the third is five pages long. If all the information that needed publicizing had been put into a single story, it would have been over ten pages. Too long!

The trend in recent years, especially in newspaper writing, but even in magazine articles, has been to shorter and shorter pieces. If a subject requires larger treatment, then the preferred approach has been to do several short, related, but still stand-alone pieces, each one emphasizing a different aspect of the bigger story.

- Release #1 is a general background article about TeleDirect and what it does. Of the three, it could most easily stand alone. However, it lacks specific detail.
- Release #2, although it says some of the same things to be found in #1, emphasizes the specific benefits of the TeleDirect system from the user's point of view.
- Release #3 is by far the most technically oriented of the three, going into specifics of the system's hardware and software. Of the three, this one would be the least likely to be used by a newspaper because of its more technical approach, but *is* of interest to trade publications.
- The captions were designed to reinforce major points made in the articles and were written so that virtually any of the pictures could be used with any of the articles.

TeleDirect Release #1

NEWS RELEASE—At will

TELEDIRECT'S UNIQUE APPROACH

DAVENPORT, IOWA—There are two ways to design a computer-aided telemarketing system.

One way is to marvel at all the "gee whiz" stuff computers can do—like collect lots of numbers and cross-tabulate them six ways from Sunday—and then build a system with loads of number-crunching capabilities.

Another way is to ask the fundamental question "What do tele-marketers want most?"

Come up with the answer "More contacts per telemarketing agent in less time."

And then design a system from scratch that delivers more contacts per telemarketing agent in less time, that allows telemarketers to do more of what they do best – talk to people!

That's how one of the founders of TeleDirect International, of Davenport, Iowa, approached it, according to Kathleen M. Kelly, President.

"The earliest concepts for what eventually became TeleDirect were the ideas of a telemarketing manager, not a computer whiz," she says. "He wanted more sales. It's just that simple."

He had noticed that his telemarketing agents were spending only about a third of their time actually talking to someone on the other end of the line, she said. The rest of the time they were dialing, listening to busy signals and disconnect recordings, or just plain waiting for someone to answer.

One of the earliest givens of the TeleDirect system was that it would use an unprecedented *three* lines per telemarketing agent station, she said.

"The rationale was, if a telemarketing agent is spending only one-third of the time actually talking to someone, then why not give the agent three times as many chances to talk to someone?" Kelly said.

The earliest experimental TeleDirect system used a VIC 20 processor with an off-the-shelf tape recorder for data storage. Later a Commodore 64 replaced the VIC. In today's version the command center is a PC/AT computer with proprietary hardware driving the telemarketing stations.

Research and development took roughly three years, Kelly said, from 1983 to 1986. The first prototype system, a CTS 515, was installed in the *Quad-City Times* (Davenport, Ia.) subscription telemarketing room in 1985.

In April 1987, TeleDirect introduced the CTS 515 and installed six systems. In September 1987, it offered CAT(TM), and, as of the end of March 1988, had installed twenty-five systems.

Kelly said TeleDirect is now at work on CAT II(TM) and expects to have it available in the marketplace by the end of 1988.

# # #

SEE ATTACHED PHOTO PACKET

FOR MORE INFO:

TeleDirect International
736 Federal St.
Davenport, Ia. 52803
   319/324-7720

TeleDirect Release #2

NEWS RELEASE—At will

TELEDIRECT'S CAT (TM) SYSTEM DELIVERS
MORE CONTACTS PER TELEMARKETING AGENT

DAVENPORT, IOWA—One of the givens that drove the earliest designs of TeleDirect International's CAT(TM) telemarketing system was that it had to deliver more actual customer contacts per telemarketing agent in less time.

According to Kathleen M. Kelly, President of TeleDirect International, Davenport, Iowa, "Telemarketing is a numbers game. The more people a telemarketing agent can talk to in an hour, the more sales will be made.

"But for years the outbound telemarketing industry assumed it was not humanly possible to make more than thirty or forty call attempts per hour, even with so-called automatic dialers," she says.

Yet, says Kelly, TeleDirect's CAT(TM) system routinely delivers:

- Up to 200 call attempts per hour.

- And up to sixty to seventy actual contacts per hour, depending on the type of list being used.

But is this how it works in the real world?

According to Dan Janovetz, President of Tele-Sales Systems, Phoenix, Ariz., who does subscription telemarketing for the Phoenix *Republic* and *Gazette,* after installing a TeleDirect CAT(TM) system, "We found a substantial improvement in sales per hour."

In fact, he said, "For the average telemarketing agent a doubling of sales was common, and some of our real stars actually hit quadruple the number of sales."

It only takes an hour or so to learn how to use the CAT system, Janovetz said. "Once they got the hang of it, our telemarketing agents were hooked on the system because they understood it meant the potential for more sales in less time," he added.

Mike Proebstle, Sales and Promotion Manager for the St. Petersburg *Times,* reports similar results after installing a Tele-Direct CAT(TM) system in their subscription telemarketing operation in early December 1987.

"We're very pleased with the system. It improved our productivity immensely, in some cases up to threefold," Proebstle said. "The telemarketing agents like the system because it's easy to use and because they get more sales and make more money."

According to Kelly, between August 1987, when the TeleDirect CAT(TM) system was introduced, and the end of March 1988, they've had installations in and/or orders from nearly two dozen of the top 100 newspaper subscription telemarketing departments in the United States, including the *Rocky Mountain News* in Denver (CO), the Boston (MA) *Globe,* the Chicago (IL) *Sun-Times,* the

Tampa (FL) *Tribune*, the Oakland (CA) *Tribune*, and the Phoenix (AZ) *Republic* and *Gazette*.

# # #

SEE ATTACHED PHOTO PACKET

FOR MORE INFO:

TeleDirect International
736 Federal St.
Davenport, Ia. 52803
  319/324-7720

TeleDirect Release #3

NEWS RELEASE—At will

TELEDIRECT INTERNATIONAL'S
CAT(TM) SYSTEM WAS DESIGNED "BACKWARDS"

DAVENPORT, IOWA—TeleDirect International's unique CAT (TM) telemarketing hardware/software system was designed "backwards," according to Jon Higby, Technical Director for the Davenport, Iowa-based firm.

"We asked ourselves: What capabilities do out-bound telemarketing agents need right at the station to do their job better, which is to spend more time in customer contact? Then we designed the hardware and software for the CAT(TM) backwards from the telemarketing agents' viewpoint," Higby says.

For instance, one fundamental difference between TeleDirect's CAT(TM) system and most other computer-based telemarketing systems is that each telemarketing agent's station can dial and monitor three outbound lines simultaneously, he says.

"With most single-line per station systems, even if they use speed dialers, the telemarketing agent still spends too much time waiting for the phone to be answered. We tried to design TeleDirect's CAT(TM) to maximize opportunities for the agent to be in contact with a live person," Higby said.

A TeleDirect CAT(TM) system's telemarketing agent's station includes:

- An RGB color monitor, which tells the agent at a glance the phone number, name, address, and special information for each number being worked, the current status of each number (dialing, ringing, on line, transferred to another agent), and data on the station performance (call attempts, contacts, sales, on-line time, and total time).

- A special-function call control panel that can dial and monitor three outbound telephone lines simultaneously. The special functions include:

   o Call connection and transfer keys.
   o Contact codes (sale/no sale and redial).
   o Noncontact codes (disconnect, answering machine, busy, and improper dial).
   o Call supervisor key.
   o A standard twelve-button touch dialing pad.

- Three line monitors.
- A headset with microphone for the operator.

But how do working telemarketing agents feel about TeleDirect's CAT(TM) system?

According to Mike Proebstle, Sales and Promotion Manager for the St. Petersburg, Fla., *Tribune,* who installed the CAT(TM) system in his subscription telemarketing operation in early December 1987, "Our agents like it because it's simple to work with and increases their productivity, which means they make more."

"You don't need to be computer-literate to operate the telemarketing agents' station or even the supervisor's command center," says Dan Janovetz, President of Tele-Sales Systems, Inc., Phoenix, Ariz.

According to Higby, an initial TeleDirect CAT(TM) system typically includes five stations controlling fifteen lines, a master control unit, and supervisor's monitor and markets for about $45,000. The maximum number of telemarketing agent stations per system is sixteen, controlling forty-eight lines.

A TeleDirect CAT(TM) system's supervisor's station includes:

- A PC/AT computer with custom boards and CAT(TM) software.
- A color monitor, full PC keyboard, printer, and backup tape drive.
- A supervisor's monitor.

The CAT(TM) system's master control unit includes computerized dialing modules, telephone circuitry, programmed chips, and station computers.

The CAT(TM) system's software includes:

- Mainframe interface.
- Flexible construction of dialing files, including random dialing of an entire exchange or working targeted soft lists.
- Maintenance of current lists, including "do not call" flagging and automatic duplicate search.
- Daily, weekly, and monthly reports, including status of individual telemarketing agent stations, status by project, number of contacts and contact time per agent, closings and closing rate, redials, deletes, busy, no answers, answering machines, and disconnects.
- Automatic redial of busy signals and no answers coded by hour so that they can be tried later.

According to Higby, TeleDirect International is working on CAT II(TM), which they hope to introduce in 1988. It is expected to include new features like an optical scanner automatically transferring lists from hard copy, expandability to thirty-two stations with ninety-six lines, and optional on-line order capability.

# # #

SEE ATTACHED PHOTO PACKET

FOR MORE INFO:

TeleDirect International
736 Federal St.
Davenport, Ia. 52803
319/324-7720

TeleDirect International Photo Packet

With the TeleDirect CAT(TM) system, each telemarketing agent's station can automatically dial three outbound lines simultaneously. The color monitor provides an at-a-glance report of the names and addresses of numbers being worked, as well as the current status of each (ringing, on line, transferred to another agent).

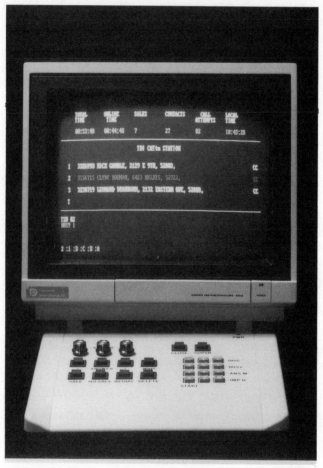

The basic TeleDirect CAT(TM) system includes five telemarketing agent stations, a command center, and a master control unit. The system can handle up to sixteen stations. Each station includes a monitor, special-function call control panel, three line monitors, and an operator headset with microphone.

The TeleDirect CAT(TM) system command center includes a color monitor, PC/AT, hard drive, printer, and CAT(TM) software. It can interface with a main-frame, construct flexible dialing files, and deliver daily, weekly, and monthly reports on the status of an individual telemarketing agent's stations, as well as project totals.

The basic assumption behind the CAT(TM) system, to deliver more on-line time to each telemarketing agent, was designed from the perspective of a telemarketing operator, not a computer whiz, according to Kathleen M. Kelly, TeleDirect International's President and CEO.

The TeleDirect CAT(TM) system is very "user friendly." Each tele-marketing agent's station features a simple-to-use call control panel that includes volume setting, call waiting, call transfer, and a standard twelve-button dial pad. Most agents get the hang of it with less than two hours training.

II: BLACKHAWK FOUNDRIES

The following is an illustration of the kind of routine news release that many small businesses should be sending out. It announces several job changes, including a couple of promotions.

It is sent out for two reasons. First, it reminds the community of the company in a positive way; basically it says that it is growing and creating new jobs. Second, it acknowledges publicly that the people named in the article are valued employees—which is great for their egos.

This news release was sent to local newspapers and to one out-of-town trade publication. The release that went to the local daily newspapers included an individual head-and-shoulders, professionally shot photo of each of the four people named in the release, and all these were used on the business page.

Blackhawk Release #1

FOR RELEASE AT WILL

BLACKHAWK ANNOUNCES STAFF CHANGES

Blackhawk Foundries, Davenport, Ia., has announced the following personnel changes, according to Jim Grafton, Jr., vice-president of manufacturing:

- Dick Ocar, Bettendorf, has been promoted to general sales manager of Blackhawk Foundries. Ocar has worked in Blackhawk's sales department for six years and has spent his entire career in the foundry industry.

- Ted Taber, Rock Island, has been appointed quality control manager. An ASQC-certified quality engineer, Taber was formerly with Cat's Davenport Plant, where he was responsible for developing SPC seminars for employees and vendors. He has a strong background in Juran, Taguchi, and NSST. Taber holds a masters degree from Northern Illinois University, Dekalb.

- Lyle Heberling, Eldrige, has been named plant metallurgist. He received his bachelor's degree in metallurgy and materials engineering from Lehigh University, Bethlehem, Pa. in 1983. Before joining Blackhawk, he worked for the GMC truck central foundry in Pontiac, Mich., where he was cupola and sand lab supervisor.

  - Jerry Kenney, Kewanee, has been named Blackhawk's core room superintendent. Previously he has worked as the quality control manager at Walworth Foundry, Kewanee, and as a core room supervisor at the John Deere Foundry, East Moline.

# # #

MORE INFO:

Jim Grafton, Vice-President, 319/323-3621
Blackhawk Foundries
323 S. Clark
Davenport, Ia. 52802

III: RAILS TO THE FAIR

This is a typical example of the type of news release known as an advance, one that announces an upcoming event. It was sent to all the local media. One of the local papers and one of the TV stations contacted the Rails to the River people and each did larger pieces.

Rails Release

NEWS RELEASE—For immediate release

THIS YEAR "ROCKET" TO THE IOWA STATE FAIR

If the monotony of the three-hour drive from the Quad-Cities to Des Moines on I-80 is about as exciting a prospect as listening to grass grow ...

Then next month you'll have the chance to get to Des Moines in a truly unique fashion—by train. Something you haven't been able to do in nearly two decades!

One-day "Rocket to the Fair" excursions from Rock Island to the Iowa State Fair have been scheduled for Saturday, Aug. 20, and Sunday, Aug. 21.

The train will follow the old Rock Island Line tracks across eastern Iowa that were once part of the Rock Island's famed Denver Rocket, hence the "Rocket to the Fair" name. The tracks are currently part of the Iowa Interstate Railroad system.

Adult round-trip tickets are $49.50 and tickets for children under 11 are $39.50. Included is the round trip from the Quad-Cities to Des Moines and general admission to the Iowa State Fair. Snack and beverage service will be available on the train.

The excursions will depart from the old Rock Island Line depot at 31st St. and 5th Ave., Rock Island, at 7 A.M. both days, will stop in Iowa City at 8:30, and will arrive in Des Moines at 11:30.

Saturday's return trip will depart Des Moines at 7 P.M. and arrive in Rock Island at 11:30 P.M. Sunday's excursion will leave Des Moines at 5:30 P.M. and arrive in Rock Island at 10 P.M.

Tickets may be purchased at six Quad-Cities Eagle Food Stores—902 W. Kimberly Rd. and 2357 W. Locust St., Davenport; 2850 18th St., Bettendorf; 2252 24th St., Rock Island; 4401 16th St., Moline; 1000 W. 4th St., Milan—and at the Davenport, Bettendorf, and Illinois Quad-Cities Chambers of Commerce.

The two "Rocket to the Fair" excursions are being sponsored by the Chicago-based 20th Century Railroad Club, with the cooperation of the Iowa Association of Railroad Passengers, Iowa City.

The 20th Century Railroad Club is a nonprofit group of several thousand railroad enthusiasts from throughout the northern Midwest. They will provide the passenger cars for the excursions from private sources. All cars will be air-conditioned and the train will be diesel-powered.

The Iowa Association of Railroad Passengers, Inc., also a nonprofit group of railroad buffs, is supplying volunteers to staff the two excursions.

The Rock Island Connection to the Quad-Cities, Ltd., partners Rose Ann Hass and Pam Siegert of Rock Island, are handling Quad-Cities ticket sales for the "Rocket to the Fair" excursions.

This year's Iowa State Fair theme is "An Old-Fashioned Good Time." The International Pro Rodeo is the grandstand attraction Aug. 20 and 21.

# # #

FOR MORE INFORMATION:
Rock Island Connection
3716 14th St.
Rock Island, Ill. 61201
  309/786-7533

APPENDIX
B

Supplemental Reading

The Complete Book of Product Publicity, James D. Barhydt (New York: AMACOM, 1987).

Crisis Management, Steven Fink (New York: AMACOM, 1986).

Handbook for Public Relations Writing, Thomas Bivins (Lincolnwood, Ill.: NTC Business Books, 1988).

How to Get Publicity, William Parkhurst (New York: Times Books, 1985).

Publicity, Ted Klein and Fred Danzig (New York: Scribner, 1985).

Public Relations & Publicity Style Book (Philadelphia: Ayer Press, 1979).

Public Relations for the Entrepreneur and the Growing Business, Norman R. Soderberg (Chicago: Probus Publishing Co., 1986).

Public Relations/Publicity, Louis B. Ehrenkranz and Gilbert R. Kahn (New York: Fairchild Publications, 1983).

Public Relations Writing, Kerry Tucker and Doris Derelian (Engelwood Cliffs, N.J.: Prentice-Hall, 1989).

Talking Back to the Media, Peter Hannaford (New York: Facts on File Publications, 1986).

Trend Watching, John E. Merriam and Joe Makower (New York: Tilden Press/AMACOM, 1988).

APPENDIX
C

Glossary

Over the years the people involved in public relations and the media have developed a special jargon. Understanding their terms can help you communicate more clearly with professionals in the field, can help establish your credibility as a practitioner, and can aid in your planning and evaluation programs.

As in other industries, many familiar words have taken on special or more limited meanings within the communications and public relations fields. The following glossary supplies definitions of terms only as they are used in the context of journalism, public relations, and communications.

action shot A photograph, film clip, or video sequence that shows action or activity.

actuarial Generally used in radio to refer to a tape-recorded comment or statement issued by a politician or other official spokesperson.

ad rate How much a medium charges for paid advertising space or time.

advance A news release issued to announce an upcoming event.

advertising Space in a newspaper or magazine and/or airtime on a TV or radio station for which a sponsor has paid a fee in order to have a particular message delivered.

advertorial A contraction of "advertising" and "editorial," generally used in the print media to designate paid advertising that has been structured to appear like editorial material.

angle The unique element of a news release or news story that will capture the interest of the reader or viewer; also *hook, peg,* or *slant.*

area of dominant influence (ADI) An electronic media term defining the market area served by TV or radio stations. It is normally stated in terms of one or more counties.

attribution Reporters must generally attribute information they use to a source, preferably a specifically named person, identified by title.

audience Term used by the electronic media to designate their viewers and listeners, and by public relations people to mean the specific group they are trying to reach with their publicity programs.

B&W Black and white photograph.

backgrounder A kind of news release used to give specific and detailed background information on an issue, a company or organization, a product or service. It is usually, but not always, part of a media kit.

beat The specific specialty area a reporter covers, such as the political beat, the health beat, or the police beat.

billboard Sometimes used in TV to refer to a visual element flashed on the screen that relates to the story being told, as for example, a graphic of a fire engine during a story about a local house fire.

bio Short for a biography, an article usually supplied as part of a media kit.

blowup A photo enlargement.

book Often used as a synonym for magazine.

booking Getting an appearance date as a guest on a talk show.

brainstorming A group discussion technique in which a specific problem or goal is defined and then ideas are aired in a freewheeling, unstructured manner.

brief A short, routine article. Business briefs, for instance, are announcements of promotions, personnel changes, and new hires that generally run on the business page.

broadcasting Programming sent over the airwaves by the traditional electronic media, such as radio and television, to large, undifferentiated audiences as opposed to *narrowcasting*.

broadsheet The traditional and still the most common newspaper format. Broadsheet page dimensions are normally close to twice those of a tabloid page.

byline The name of the author of a story or article, usually appearing at the top of the first page.

cable TV Television signals that are delivered to the home by cable rather than over the airwaves; it is normally characterized by a broad range of channels, including many from outside the immediate market, and multiple programming choices.

camera ready A term applied to an advertisement, news article, or photograph that is ready to be placed directly on a newspaper or magazine layout page just prior to going to camera, without any typesetting or other preparation.

campaign   A planned program of publicity, often used in conjunction with other promotion techniques, to accomplish specific goals.

circulation   The number of copies a newspaper or magazine distributes to its readers. *Paid* circulation means that readers have paid something to receive the publication; the post office, as well as most circulation auditing agencies, require that the payment be more than nominal. *Free* circulation generally means that the publication is distributed without charge either by carrier, bulk mail, or at pickup points.

city desk   A key decision point in the editorial hierarchy of most newspapers; see *city editor.*

city editor   The editor responsible for most of the local news coverage by a newspaper. City editors assign reporters to specific stories and decide how and where stories will be played.

classified ad   A newspaper or magazine advertisement that contains strictly text material (no drawings, photos, or logos) and that usually appears in its own special section of the publication.

clip   This word has many variations in the communications field. *Clip art* refers to notebooks that contain a variety of generic drawings, photographs, borders, and other graphics typically used in ads to attract attention. You'll often hear the word "clip" used as a synonym for article, as in "Get me the clip on that school board controversy." Similarly, the TV media will often use "clip" as an abbreviation of *filmclip,* a short sequence on film or videotape. A *clip service* is an agency that will read designated publications and clip articles according to your specifications. Finally, radio people will sometimes use "clip" as shorthand for *soundclip,* a short recording.

cold type   A photographically based method of setting type, the method most commonly used by today's publications. By contrast with the old-fashioned method that involved melted lead called "hot type," it is both faster and more cost-effective.

column   A bylined article of opinion or analysis published on a more or less regular basis. It can be nationally syndicated or locally written.

column inch   A basic measurement in newspapers, one column wide by one inch deep. Newspaper ad sizes and ad rates are normally quoted in terms of column inches.

commentary   An opinion on or analysis of some current issue during a TV or radio news broadcast; see *editorial.*

community calendar   Brief announcements, usually grouped together, of upcoming events or activities given by both the electronic and print media.

community paper A newspaper, usually published less often than daily, that serves the specific information needs of a smaller and/or rural community; it rarely carries nonlocal news.

contact A source of information for a news story.

contact sheet A "proof" of small black and white versions of all photographs taken in a given shoot, the best of which are selected for publication.

copy Term used by reporters to refer to their written articles or stories, as in handing in "copy" to an editor. A*d copy* is the narrative part of a print ad or the script for an electronic media ad.

credit line The source of an illustration or the name of the photographer who shot a picture, similar to a byline.

daily A newspaper published on a daily basis, five days, six days, or seven days a week.

dateline The city of origin of a story, usually appearing in all caps at the beginning of the first paragraph.

deadline The time by which a publication or an electronic medium must have material in order for it to be used in its next edition or newscast.

desktop publishing Personal computer-based systems that will set type, place written materials in columns, and insert graphics or illustrations, all electronically.

display ad An ad in a newspaper or magazine that makes use of copy blocks, open space, illustrations, and logos, as opposed to a classified ad.

dot matrix A system in many computer printers that uses small dots to form letters and/or graphic elements; sending dot matrix printed news releases should be avoided, as they are sometimes difficult to read.

double-spaced Typing style in which a blank line appears between each line of type, as opposed to single-spaced pages. All news releases should be double-spaced.

editor Overall term applied to many positions in both the print and electronic media. The *assignment editor* on a TV or radio news operation assigns specific reporters to specific story assignments; a *copy editor* edits copy, writes headlines, and dummies (designs) pages in the print media; a *features editor* is in charge of assigning and editing feature stories, such as personality profiles, entertainment articles, or food features; the *editor-in-chief* is in charge of the entire news operation at a print medium, while the *managing editor* makes most of the day-to-day decisions; a *section editor* is responsible for certain sections of a print medium, such as the business page.

editorial   An opinion on or analysis of some current issue; generally unsigned, it is considered the policy of the publication; see *commentary.*

evening edition   The edition of a newspaper that is issued in the late afternoon.

evening news   A TV station's major daily news program broadcast in the early evening, usually around the dinner hour.

exclusive   An important news story that one medium has all to itself; also known as a *scoop.*

fact sheet   A form of background news release normally found in media kits that simply lists facts about the business or group.

fam tour   Short for "familiarization" tour, an organized visit to a tourism area, a military installation, or industrial facility arranged specifically for the media; also known as a *junket.*

fax   Short for "facsimile," the sending of written information over telephone lines by converting the typewritten letters to digital impulses. It is most often used as a noun: "We just got this fax in from the senator's office." But it can also be used as a verb: "Fax this to the West Coast office right away."

feature story   An article in a newspaper or magazine that differs in both writing style and content from the material appearing in the regular news columns.

Federal Communications Commission (FCC)   The U.S. government agency that regulates the electronic media and issues their operating licenses.

file film   Usually actual videotape of past news stories that can be used to illustrate a current story.

five-day paper   A newspaper published weekdays, Monday through Friday.

follow-up interview   A one-on-one interview of a news source after a news conference.

follow-up release   A news release issued after an event to report the results of that event.

free lance   Term applied to writers who write articles for or supply material to a medium but who are not regular members of that medium's staff; they are usually paid a flat fee for each project.

frequency   An electronic media term referring to the expected number of times a given individual will see a specific ad message.

general manager   The CEO of a radio or TV station.

glossy   A photo print, usually, but not always, black and white.

grab 'n' grin   A derisive term used by the media to refer to check presentations and other staged publicity events.

guest editorial   An editorial column written by an outside expert who is not part of the publication's regular staff.

H&S   Short for head and shoulders, referring to the small photos often used in print media.

halftone   A photograph that has been converted from a glossy print to a format a newspaper, magazine, or other print medium can reproduce; also called *PMT.*

headline   The words at the top of a newspaper or magazine article that tell the reader what the story is about; the *banner headline* is the major headline at the top or near the top of page one of most newspapers.

home edition   The edition of a newspaper for delivery to homes; other editions include the *street edition* (for newsstand sales) and the *state* or *regional edition* (for rural areas).

house ad   Usually a display ad run in a newspaper or magazine at no charge on behalf of some charitable agency or community goal. It is analogous to the electronic media's public service announcements (PSAs).

house organ   A publication issued internally by a business or organization for its employees and/or customers.

image   The specific positive feelings and attitudes you want the reader and/or viewer to have about your organization.

influentials   Persons who are of particular importance to your organization because they can have a major influence on its future course. They can include political figures, business or community leaders, regulators, key customers, key suppliers, and others.

junket   Similar to a fam tour.

keyline   Also known as *pasteup*, the affixing in final position of type, photographs, and other visual elements on pages exactly as they will appear in print. It can be used as either a noun or a verb, depending on the context.

late news   The late evening television news, usually broadcast around 10 or 11 P.M.

lead   The first paragraph of a newspaper article, which, by tradition, always includes the most important element(s) of the story.

letter to the editor   A letter of opinion written to a newspaper, magazine, or other medium intended for publication.

library   A publication's files of back issues and of other useful articles or clips; also known as *morgue.*

live   An interview of a news source conducted live on the air, that is, not tape-recorded earlier for broadcast during the news later.

lobby   To try to influence legislation; a *lobbyist* is one who lobbies.

local access channel   Usually a cable channel, sometimes an over-the-air channel, sponsored by a college or other group, designed specifically for public service programming by local groups about local issues.

local origination   Term used to describe a program originated by a local station, as opposed to one originated by a network.

logo   A distinctive symbol and/or type style used to identify one specific organization, brand, or product.

magazine   A print medium issued periodically (usually weekly or monthly) that has a specific editorial and audience focus.

mailing list   A list of the names and addresses of people you wish to reach; it can be either a list you have gathered or one you acquired from someone else.

major media   The newspaper(s), television and radio stations in a given market, also known as *mass media*.

media advisory   Either a stand-alone news release or an addition to a news release that gives the media special information, such as a news conference schedule or how to obtain media credentials for an event.

media event   Any event staged specifically for the media that is designed to generate publicity for an individual or group; see also *news conference*.

media file   A file of information kept on particular media and including such items as contact names, addresses and phone numbers, and deadlines.

media kit   A collection of several stories about an individual or organization used to provide background information to the media.

media plan   A written plan for how an organization will develop various types of publicity through specific media.

media tour   See *fam tour* and *junket*.

modem   A device that allows computers to "talk" directly to one another over regular telephone lines.

morning edition   A newspaper that is normally delivered to homes or newsstands early in the morning.

mugshot   A small head-and-shoulders photograph of a news maker or personality.

narrowcasting   What cable TV and other electronic media do when they specifically target their programming at small market segments, as opposed to *broadcasting*.

neighborhood paper Usually a free but sometimes a paid-circulation newspaper that specializes in news and information about a specific neighborhood or group.

network The affiliation of television or radio stations to receive and/or generate programming on a regional or national basis.

network affiliate A local station that is part of a network.

news conference A news event to which all media are invited so that they can hear a major announcement and/or ask questions of an important news maker; also known as a *press conference.*

news director The person in charge of the news operation at a television or radio station.

newsletter A publication issued periodically (biweekly, monthly, or quarterly) and directed at a very narrowly defined audience.

newspaper A publication issued periodically (daily or weekly) and written for a broad range of information interests in a given community or geographic area.

news release Information in written form released to all the media in the same form and at the same time; also known as a *press release.*

news trailer A written weathercast or other news bulletin that runs across the bottom of a TV screen while the regular programming continues.

obit Short for obituary, information published in a newspaper about a recently dead person.

off the record Information that a news source asks the media not to use as a direct quotation.

on the record Information that can be attributed by name to a source.

pasteup See *keyline.*

personality Sometimes used in broadcast media to designate a news source who has widespread name recognition.

photo opportunity A kind of news event that is set up specifically to provide the print media photographers and/or television cameras with something visually interesting.

PMT See *halftone.*

points The unit of measurement used for typesize in the print media, with 14 points to the inch. The higher the point size, the larger the type.

position Depending on the context, "position" can refer to an individual's or organization's stand on a particular issue; it can be the overall editorial thrust of a publication; or it can be the particular image of an individual or organization.

press   The reporters, editors, and news directors of the print and electronic media; also known as the *media*.

press release   See *news release*.

producer   In the electronic media, the person who puts the show together, decides on its format, arranges for guests, picks discussion topics, and so on.

product bulletin   A kind of news release that focuses on the technical specifications of a product or process; its use is normally limited to trade publications.

public affairs program   A discussion or documentary show on a community topic or issue run by the electronic media.

public broadcasting   Nonprofit, usually educationally oriented television and radio stations.

publicity   Any form of nonpaid exposure your business or group receives in the media, as opposed to advertising, which must be paid for.

public relations   A broad spectrum of activities designed to present your business or group in a positive manner, such as publicity, speeches, sponsoring shows and exhibits, holding open houses, publishing brochures and newsletters.

public service announcement (PSA)   A free ad or announcement on television or radio on behalf of a nonprofit group, analogous to house ads run by the print media.

publisher   The CEO of a newspaper, who normally has little to do with day-to-day news operations.

Q&A   A question and answer technique sometimes used to structure a background news release.

query letter   A letter sent to a public service show producer outlining an idea for an appearance on that show.

rate card   A summary of the official advertising rates charged by a newspaper, magazine, radio, or TV station.

rating   A radio station's, television station's, or specific show's audience share relative to that gained by other stations or shows.

reach   The number of persons who are likely to hear or see a given message during a given period of time on the electronic media.

regional edition   A newspaper edition designed for distribution to non-local areas; also known as a *state edition*.

release   Short for news release.

release date   The date and/or time after which a news item can be aired or printed.

rewrite   The editing of a news release to fit the particular needs of a specific medium.

satellite feed   The sending and/or receiving of news via satellite.

scoop   What one medium has when it runs a story that none of its rivals have; also known as an *exclusive*.

separation   Short for color separation, a process for separating the elements of a color photograph or transparency so that it can be printed in color.

seven-day paper   A newspaper published seven days a week.

share   A particular station's or program's percentage of the radio or TV sets in use at a given time.

six-day paper   A newspaper published Monday through Saturday.

slant   see *angle*.

slick   A camera-ready ad or news release on "slick" paper usually provided by a product manufacturer.

slide   A specialized form of color photography, preferred by some print media for color reproduction; also known as a *transparency*.

slugline   A one- or two-word identification or title used at the top of the second page (along with a page number) and subsequent pages of a news release.

sound bite   A brief recording of a news source's voice most often used in radio news reports.

source   The originator of news information.

special sections   More or less self-contained sections of print media in which ads and editorial content are devoted to a specific topic.

specialty media   Print or broadcast media directed at the information needs of a particular target audience, as contrasted with the mass media.

spokesperson   The official source for information about an organization.

spot   An ad on the electronic media, such as a 30-second spot.

stand-up   When a TV reporter appears on camera at the scene of a story, as in, "Mike will do a stand-up from the site of your new building."

statement   A specialized form of news release containing the "official" words of a news source.

station   A specific electronic medium, normally identified by its call letters or its channel number.

still   Slang for photograph.

stringer   Someone who furnishes news articles and/or tips to out-of-town media, but who is not part of the staff. Like free lancers, stringers are normally paid on a per item basis.

street edition   Usually the latest edition of a newspaper off the press, and intended for sale through newsstands and coin boxes.

stylebook   A manual containing the specialized rules of grammar, punctuation, and style that govern journalistic writing.

suburban paper   A newspaper published for one or more adjacent suburbs of a large urban area.

syndicate   An agency that sells articles, such as syndicated columns, to print media and programs to electronic media.

tabloid   A smaller newspaper format than that of the broadsheet used by many small community papers and by those in large urban areas that favor a more strident style of news coverage.

talk show   In the electronic media, a term used to describe various formats of guest and host interview shows; talk shows also sometimes offer some form of audience interaction.

talking head   Electronic media slang for visual elements that are confined to a spokesperson talking to reporters.

tape   Used in various ways by the electronic media: *Audiotape* records sound only; *videotape* records pictures as well as sound. Professionals in TV prefer to use a one-inch-wide format to record news events and other programming because of its higher quality; smaller, Beta and VHS formats are used by home video cameras and recorders.

target audience   The specific group you wish to reach with your publicity message; the more specifically defined this group is, the better.

think piece   Media slang for a usually lengthy article or news item that stresses analysis and background information.

30   The traditional signal for the end of a news release, which can also be indicated by three pound signs, "**###**," or simply by "END."

tickler file   A system for reminding yourself of important deadlines or activities in the future.

tracking   Various methods for measuring and evaluating the coverage a specific medium or group of media is giving to one or more topics.

trade publication   A newspaper or magazine published for the specific information needs of a certain industry or subgroup of an industry.

typo   Typographical error or misspelled word.

VCR   Videocassette recorder.

visuals   The drawings, photographs, demonstrations, maps, charts, film clips, or other elements in a media kit or at a news conference that provide visual variety for the media.

weekly   A newspaper published on a weekly basis and normally serving a small community or rural area.

wire service   A national or worldwide news gathering agency, the best known wire services being the Associated Press (AP) and United Press International (UPI).

Index